Courage and Co ...uice

Courage and Cowardice

◆

The Liberation Of Kuwait And The Rape Of Basra

Delbert N. Abbott

iUniverse, Inc.

New York Lincoln Shanghai

Courage and Cowardice
The Liberation Of Kuwait And The Rape Of Basra

iUniverse books may be ordered through booksellers or by contacting:

iUniverse
2021 Pine Lake Road, Suite 100
Lincoln, NE 68512
www.iuniverse.com
1-800-Authors (1-800-288-4677)

ISBN: 0-595-33430-X (pbk)
ISBN: 0-595-66924-7 (cloth)

Printed in the United States of America

This book is dedicated to my wife Kim for her love and support in the writing of this personal history and to those who gave the ultimate sacrifice during Desert Shield and Desert Storm.

Contents

Introduction

This book is being written to honor and remember those soldiers of Desert Shield and Desert Storm who were killed during the conflict. We tend to remember General Powell, General Schwarzkopf, and the others who lead us to victory in the Gulf. But if it weren't for the soldiers listed in this book, and others like them who put their lives on the line for their country, those Generals would have been nothing more than overpaid chess players.

Recorded are the names of those killed during Desert Shield and Desert Storm so that each time this book is read these soldiers will be remembered for their sacrifice. It would be almost impossible to relate all of the stories surrounding the lives of those who gave the ultimate sacrifice. But if they could be recorded, the result would comprise many books and touch us all very deeply. All I can do is let you know a first-hand account of what it was like for me and my platoon for the five months we were deployed to the Middle East during Operation Desert Shield and Desert Storm. Perhaps by reading this account you will be able to get a flavor of how it was on the front lines, where there were no cameras.

Those Who Gave The Ultimate Sacrifice

Air Force Major Barry Henderson, 40.
Air Force Major Stephen Scramm, 43.
Army Sergeant Arthur Jackson, 36.
Marine Sergeant Larry Hogan, 33.
Navy Petty Officer Timothy Jackson, 20.
Marine Lt. Col. James Cunningham, 42.
Air Force Staff Sergeant John Campisi, 30.
Air Force Capt. James Poulet, 34.
Air Force Major Peters S. Hook, 36.
Marine Corporal Timothy W. Romei, 22.
Navy Petty Officer Andrew T. Cady, 25.
Marine Lt. James H. Love, 31.
Navy Petty Officer Michael L. Belliveau, 24.

Air Force Staff Sergeant Marc Cleyman, 30.
Air Force Tech Sergeant Daniel G. Perez, 50.
Army 2nd Lt. Shannon Kelley, 23.
Navy Petty Officer Delwin Delgado, 26.
Navy Boatswain's Mate Marvin Plummer, 27.
Navy Specialist Nathaniel H. Kemp, 18.
Navy Petty Officer Phillip L. Wilkinson, 35.
Navy Airman Larry M. Clark, 21.
Navy Airman Apprentice Christopher B. Brown, 19.
Navy Clerk Timothy B. Seay, 22.
Marine Captain William Cronin, Jr., 29.
Marine Captain William J. Hurley, 27.
Marine Sergeant Kenneth T. Keller, 26.
Army Private First Class John W. Hutto, 19.
Army Chief Warrant Officer Robert Godfrey, 32.
Marine Capt. James N. Willbourn III, 28.
Army Sergeant David Quentin Douthit, 24.
Marine Lance Corporal Eliseo Felix, 19.
Marine Capt. Aaron A. Pack, 22.
Air Force Captain Paul R. Eichenlaub II, 29.
Army Sergeant Scotty L. Whittenburg, 22.
Army Specialist Steven G. Mason, 23.
Army Corporal J. Scott Lindsey, 27.
Army Private First Class David Mark Wieczorek, 21.
Marine Lance Corporal Thomas A. Jenkins, 20.
Army Specialist Adrienne L. Mitchell, 20.
Army Sergeant Jimmy D. Haws, 28.
Army Sergeant Edwin B. Kutz, 26.
Army Sergeant David R. Crumby, Jr., 26.
Army Private First Class David W. Kramer, 20.
Army Sergeant Adrian L. Stokes, 20.
Army Sergeant Young Dillon, 27.
Army Staff Sergeant William T. Butts, 30.
Army Specialist Cindy Beaudoin, 19.
Army Capt. James R. McCoy, 29.
Army Sergeant Dodge R. Powell, 28.
Army Chief Warrant Officer Phillip Garvey, 39.
Army Staff Sergeant Michael Robson, 30.

Army Specialist James Worthy, 22.
Marine Corporal Phillip J. Jones, 21.
Army Private First Class Robert Wade, 31.
Amy Specialist Roy Damian, Jr., 21.
Marine Lance Corporal Frank C. Allen, 22.
Army Sergeant Nels A. Moller, 23.
Marine Lance Corporal Christian J. Porter, 20.
Air Force Major Thomas F. Koritz, 37.
Army Captain Brian K. Simpson, 22.
Marine Lance Corporal Brian L. Lane, 20.
Army Specialist James R. Miller, 20.
Army Specialist Michael Mills, 23
Army Specialist Ronald D. Rennison, 21.
Army Specialist Michael Daniels, 20.
Army Corporal Jeff Middleton, 23.
Army Private First Class Marty R. Davis, 19.
Army Sergeant First Class Gary Streeter, 40.
Marine Captain Reginald Underwood, 33.
Air Force Major Donnie R. Holland, 42.
Army Sergeant Ronald M. Randazzo, 24.
Army Sergeant Russell G. Smith, Jr., 44.
Army Specialist Timothy Hill, 23.
Army Private First Class Aaron W. Howard, 20.
Army Specialist William E. Palmer, 23.
Army Corporal Stanley W. Bartusiak, 34.
Army Sergeant Roger Brilinski, 24.
Marine Lance Corporal Stephen E. Bentzlin, 23.
Army Specialist Glen D. Jones, 21.
Navy Lt. Charles J. Turner, 29.
Army Specialist Steven P. Farnen, 22.
Army Specialist Phillip D. Mobley, 26.
Navy Lt. William T. Costen, 27.
Army Warrant Officer David Plasch, 23.
Marine Sergeant Garett A. Mongrella, 25.
Army Private Robert D. Talley, 18.
Army Capt. Mario Fajardo, 29.
Marine Corporal Ismael Cotto, 27.
Army Staff Sergeant Patbouvier Ortiz, 27.

Army Master Sergeant Otto F. Clark, 35.
Army Specialist Thomas G. Stone, 20.
Marine Lance Corporal David T. Snyder, 21.
Army Staff Sergeant David Ames, 30.
Army Specialist Kenneth J. Perry, 23.
Army Sergeant Michael A. Harris, Jr. 26.
Air Force 1st Lt. Patrick B. Olson, 25.
Army Private First Class Jerry L. King, 20.
Army Specialist Clarence A. Cash, 20.
Army Specialist Anthony W. Kidd, 21.
Marine Lance Corporal James H. Lumpkins, 22.
Navy Lt. Robert J. Dwyer, 32.
Army Chief Warrant Officer Hal H. Reichle, 27.
Army Staff Sergeant Johnathan Kamm, 25.
Army Staff Sergeant Tony Applegate, 28.
Army Warrant Officer George Swartzendruber, 25.
Marine Lance Corporal Michael E. Linderman, Jr., 19.
Army Private First Class Michael C. Dailey, 19.
Army Specialist Troy Wedgwood, 22.
Army Specialist Steven Atherton, 25.
Army Specialist John Boliver, 27.
Army Specialist Joseph P. Bongiorni III, 20.
Army Sergeant John Boxler, 44.
Army Specialist Beverly Clark, 23.
Army Major Mark Connelly, 24.
Army Sergeant Alan B. Craver, 32.
Army Specialist Duane W. Hollen, Jr. 24.
Army Specialist Frank S. Keough, 22.
Army Specialist Anthony Madison, 27.
Army Specialist Christine Mayes, 22.
Army Pfc Mark A. Miller, 20.
Army Specialist Stephen J. Siko, 24.
Army Specialist Richard V. Wolverton, 24.
Army Specialist Frank J. Walls, 20.
Marine Lance Corporal James E. Waldron, 25.
Army Specialist James D. Tatum, 22.
Army Corporal Douglas L. Fielder, 22.
Army Pvt. Roger E. Valentine, 19.

Army Specialist Andy Alaniz, 20.
Army Specialist Tommy D. Butler, 22.
Air Force Captain Douglas L. Bradt, 29.
Army Specialist Melford Collins, 34.
Army Specialist Luis Delgado, 30.
Marine Sergeant James D. Hawthorne, 24.
Marine Sergeant Candelario Montalvo, 25.
Army Specialist James Murray, Jr., 20.
Army Staff Sergeant Christopher H. Stephens, 27.
Marine Lance Corporal Daniel B. Walker, 20.
Army Private First Class Corey L. Winkle, 21.
Army Staff Sergeant Harold P. Witzke III, 28.
Marine Lance Corporal Dion J. Stephenson, 22.
Army Sergeant Jason Carr, 24.
Army Sergeant Kenneth B. Gentry, 32.
Army Lt. Terry L. Plunk, 25.
Marine Lance Corporal Troy Lorrenzo Gregory, 21.
Army Corporal Jonathan M. Williams, 23.
Army Private First Class Timothy Alan Shaw, 21.
Army 1st Lt. Donaldson Tillar III, 25.
Army Major Thomas C.M. Zeugner, 36.
Army Private First Class Ardon B. Cooper, 23.
Army Sergeant Lee Belas, 22.
Army Warrant Officer John Morgan, 28.
Marine Private First Class Scott A. Schroeder, 20.
Army Sergeant William A Strehlow, 27.
Army Sergeant Brian P. Scott, 22.
Army Sergeant Cheryl LaBeau-O'Brien, 24.
Army Pvt. Michael L. Fitz, 18.
Army Specialist Manuel Davila, 22.
Army Corporal Rolando A. Delagneau, 30.
David Spellacy, 28.
Air Force Sergeant Damon V. Kanuha, 28.
Navy Lt. Commander Michael Scott Speicher, 33.
Air Force Staff Sergeant John P. Blessinger, 33.
Air Force Senior Master Sergeant Paul G. Buege, 43.
Air Force Sergeant Barry M. Clark, 26.
Air Force Capt. Arthur Galvan, 33.

Air Force Capt. William D. Grimm, 28.
Air Force Tech. Sergeant Robert K. Hodges, 28.
Air Force Master Sergeant James B. May II, 40.
Air Force Staff Sergeant John L. Oelschlager, 28.
Air Force Staff Sergeant Mark J. Schmauss, 30.
Air Force Capt. Dixon L. Walters, Jr., 29.
Air Force Major Paul J. Weaver, 34.
Air Force Capt. Stephen Richard Phillis, 30.
Air Force Staff Sergeant Timothy R. Harrison, 31.
Air Force 1st Lt. Thomas Clifford Bland, Jr., 26.
Navy Lt. Patrick K. Connor, 25.
Navy Lt. Cmdr. Barry T. Cooke, 35.
Army Specialist David Bush, 21.

This list is not complete. The web site **Gulf War Debriefing Book** (http://www.leyden.com/gulfwar/casualshield.html) was used to compile this list. Please submit corrections or additions to this web site. According to the Department Of Defense, approximately 300 American soldiers died during the war, 148 listed as combat deaths.

Secondly, I am writing this book to bring light to the decision that President H.W. Bush made reneging on his promise to support the people of Basra if they rose up to overthrow Saddam. This decision affected those of us who were in a position to see the results very deeply. President H.W. Bush promised the people of Basra that by rising against Saddams regime the United States Military would support it. Then he reneged on the promise and allowed Saddam to kill, maim and rape the citizens of Basra while we in the military watched helplessly from a distance. The Seventh Corps alone could have easily protected the people of Basra from the helicopter and ground attacks of the Iraqi army. Our presence alone moving toward Basra might have been enough to get the Iraqi Army to leave and keep the people of Basra safe. Even if the No Fly Zone had been implemented immediately after the war the people of Basra might have been spared needless tragedy.

The following is my story, a cavalry scout section sergeant who was one of the first to see the Iraqi desert west of Kuwait and make contact with the Iraqi Republican Guard unit northwest of Kuwait.

I hope that after reading this book, you will encourage your military and political leaders to be more careful in considering how our military is used and make sure they always keep their promises.

1

Prelude To A War

It was 116 degrees in the shade. There was little shade. Walking outside of the warehouse where we were living at KKMC (King Kalid Military City) was like walking near a blast furnace. After walking only fifteen feet sweat was pouring from me like condensation on the outside of a cold glass of milk on a hot day. No, I wasn't overweight. I was in the best shape of my life. I had been a part of fighting the Persian Gulf War (Desert Storm) and after months of waiting we were returning to Germany. I pictured in my mind all that we had been through and tried to make sense of it all.

In October of 1990 most of my platoon didn't believe there was even a possibility of going to the Gulf. We were stationed in Gelnhausen, Germany and our unit, 4/8 Cavalry, was scheduled to be deactivated in the near future. Our post was scheduled to be turned over to the Germans shortly thereafter. The plan was already implemented. The rear detachment was repairing broken items, painting walls and doing general cleaning. No new soldiers had been arriving and many soldiers had orders in hand to go back to the States either ETS (end time in service) or PCS (permanent change of station). The rest of us were scheduled to be piecemealed out to other units in Germany.

After Gunnery the "short timers" (soldiers who were either ETS or PCS) were so happy to be going home that they were gloating. I told them they needed to be watching the news. Other units in the States that had been scheduled to be deactivated were put on hold and their movement orders frozen. I knew that could happen to us as well. I also knew that the Army wouldn't take all the units from the States and leave the country undefended. The deciding factor would be when the country could not afford to deploy any more units from the States and there would still be units needed to attack Iraq. We would be the logical choice.

First, we were closer to the Persian Gulf than most units. Second, the fact that we were being deactivated meant that we were not needed to defend Germany. Third, once the war was over we could leave our equipment in Saudi Arabia at prepositioned equipment sites for use if we needed to go back at some later date.

One evening I was watching the news on television in the Day Room. The reporter announced that the pentagon planners had decided that more troops were needed for Desert Shield. As the reporter announced the units that were now going to be called my attention was riveted. When the Third Armored Division was announced, our Division, my mind was disbelieving. I shook my head, thinking I might not have heard correctly. The reporter repeated the units again. We were going.

My body felt like I was floating a half-inch off the floor. Something had short-circuited my nerve endings. I slowly reminded myself what I had just heard. We—are going—to the Middle East;—probably to war. Numbness covered my whole body. Quickly, my feet took me to find someone I knew to tell the news. A couple of guys from the unit came strolling down the hallway. Before I knew it I blurted out that I had just heard on the news we were going. "What", one of them said? I repeated what I had heard. They were as shocked as I. Disbelieving, they strolled down the hall toward the Day Room, shaking their heads. I went to the CQ, (charge of quarters) to let him know as well. He had been listening on Armed Forces Radio and already knew. He mentioned that even though the Third Armored Division was being deployed, maybe our brigade would not be deployed, since we were being deactivated. He pointed out the fact that we were under strength. A flicker of hope raced across my chest. Maybe he was right. We would know for sure in the next few days.

Two days later we were notified that our brigade was being deployed. All soldiers with orders were given "stop loss" instructions. No one was going home. For the next few weeks we made plans for movement to the Middle East. During this time new soldiers were assigned to us from the States. The soldiers that had been stopped from going home and the frightened new soldiers from the States soon became discipline problems. Night after night these soldiers got drunk and fought each other. Even some of the soldiers who were not in these unique groups got drunk and were late for formations. It was difficult to keep good order. I wondered how we would deploy these men in this condition yet accomplish our mission? I comforted myself with the thought that maybe, just maybe,

Saddam would be persuaded to get out of Kuwait and avoid war. I wondered if it could happen.

A few days later I was watching the news when it was announced that the Pentagon would deploy several more medical units to the Middle East. Casualties were now expected to be in the thousands if we attacked Iraq. It was too much. The shock of changing the unit from one of drawing down to one of deployment for war, morale problems, and the thought that all or some of us becoming severely wounded or dead was overwhelming. Added to this was anxiety over the fact that most of my unit, myself included, had never trained in the desert. We were used to having trees for camouflage, contours to hide behind and cool weather. In the desert we would be like sitting ducks on an ocean of sand. How would we maneuver? How would we hide? How long would it take to adapt to the desert?

I felt an overwhelming desire to escape. It seemed like we were being given a suicide mission. I checked my watch to see if my parents would be awake. The time difference made it only possible to reach them by phone for a few hours during the day. I made my way downtown to the German Post Office and waited in line to get a phone booth. As I entered the booth and shut the door I hoped that my parents could give me some insight into my situation. I hoped that they would have some sympathy and let me vent a little. My Mother answered the phone. As I began to tell her and my Dad about the deployment of more medical units I could tell there would be no sympathy. They didn't see it as anything I should be concerned about. Anyway, there was nothing I could do. My body went limp. A hot flush came over my face as tears began to roll down my cheeks. I felt embarrassed that I was not taking the situation more like a man. I couldn't imagine my Dad reacting this way.

I restrained myself so that they couldn't hear my sobs, covering the mouthpiece with my hand when I wasn't speaking. Standing in the booth, my back to the wall, I began to slide down to the floor until I was sitting on it. My body felt like dead weight. I couldn't move. The handset dangled on my shoulder as my arm slid to my lap. My parents continued to talk but I could only reply with one-word answers. The temperature in the booth seemed like someone had turned on a heater. The international operator came on the line to let us know that we had one minute left. As we said our goodbyes I felt abandoned.

As the line clicked dead I let the handset slip from my shoulder as I tried to stand. I couldn't stand. I had a vision of the men in my platoon lying in pools of blood on the desert sand screaming in agony. I pictured myself among them, glancing down to reveal that my legs were missing, my hands covered in blood. I was unable to help anyone, not even myself. It seemed so real I could feel the heat radiating from the sand and smelled burning flesh. As the handset dangled from its cord I wondered what would become of us. The conclusion was clear; there was nothing I could do but get prepared as best I could and focus on the mission ahead.

I took a look at the soldiers in my section, individualists every one of them. Anyone who thinks that soldiers are just robots just don't know the first thing about soldiers. The platoon had six Bradleys. My section consisted of two Bradleys with five soldiers each. SSG Fariello commanded another section and SFC Zettlemoyer commanded his section as well as the platoon Lt. Wynn was in overall command. In my section was SGT McCullough (Mac) commanding HQ-85. He was a very opinionated and vocal soldier who had to be reined in every so often. He was more seasoned than I when it came to knowing Bradleys. His gunner was SGT Hall, a short, stalky man with a ready smile and a quick wit. He was very energetic and got bored easily. His crew consisted of SPC McDonald as driver, with PFC Bradshaw and PFC Goss as loaders and dismounts.

My crew consisted of SGT Beets as gunner, SPC Chamberlain as driver, with SPC Allen and SPC Burns as loaders and dismounts. SGT Beets was over six feet tall with an easy manner and a warm disposition. He glided as he walked. SPC Chamberlain was a big man, too, and he loved to eat! He was a little shy, but very professional. SPC Allen had been a forest fire fighter before joining the Army. He and Burns were both a few inches shorter than I. Allen was very muscular with a ruddy face. Burns was always smiling and talked constantly. He was particular about keeping his hair looking neat and would sleep in a "dew rag".

We packed everything in our duffle bags, conexes (large metal boxes) and the Bradleys themselves. The Bradleys were put on train flatcars and headed to northern German ports. We updated our legal paperwork including wills, life insurance, and powers of attorney. A whole day was devoted to our health. The post gymnasium had medical personnel arranged behind curtained walls and portable desks.

As we snaked through the lines to receive various shots, update dog tags and check our teeth it seemed like something a dog might go through in a puppy mill. One of the shots was being administered by an air gun, instead of the standard needle and syringe. I've always hated shots, but was even more terrified of the air gun. This contraption uses forced air instead of a needle to inject the serum.

As I prepared myself to get the shot I took a quick look at the arm of the soldier two people ahead of me to see what was coming. The nurse instructed the soldier to keep still, and then, just as she injected him, he flinched. A two-inch tear ripped open the soldiers arm as blood wafted into the air. My heart raced as I kept telling myself to calm down. I shook my hands and let my arms go limp as she put the air gun to my shoulder. I thought of cool mountain streams just as the serum entered my arm and gave me a jolt. Suddenly, it was over. I felt foolish for thinking that the shot would go badly. A quiet chuckle greeted a glowing smile and a sigh of relief.

Then we waited, and waited, and waited. As Christmas approached no one could tell us if we would be in Germany or the Middle East for the holidays. We decided to celebrate it early. SFC Zettlemoyer, the Platoon Sergeant, invited those of us without families to his house and we had a good time; but it just didn't feel like Christmas.

At the morning formation on December 23rd, we were informed to have everything, including personal weapons, ready to leave at 1800 hours, 6 pm. The last thing we had to do was pack everything we weren't taking with us into boxes and place those boxes into a storage room. We were instructed to pen the names and addresses on the side of each box to the persons who we wanted to have these things if we didn't come back. As I packed memorable photographs, letters, books and other assorted personal items I couldn't help feeling like I wouldn't be coming back. In my empty room I dropped to my knees and collapsed face first onto my bunk as I finished taping shut the last box. I felt death tugging at my sleeve. I felt drained of energy, my skin felt hot and I let out a muffled sob. It was one of the toughest moments of my life.

We loaded on German tour buses as the sun was going down and headed for Rein Main Air Base. As we shuffled onto Air Force C-141's the future was very uncertain. As I took a seat pulled down from the wall of the plane I tried to gather my thoughts. I couldn't think. There were too many variables. I asked God for three things. I did not want anyone in my platoon to become injured or killed. I did not want to have to kill anyone. And I didn't want to see any dead bodies. I knew this was a tall order, coming from a combat soldier. I put everything in Gods hands. The future was his. The hum of the jet engines lulled me to sleep as we headed to an unknown future.

2

Touchdown In The desert

Upon touching down on the tarmac at the airport in Riyadh, Saudi Arabia we deplaned in semi-darkness, the night sky being lit by numerous stars. After we grabbed our duffle bags off of the pallets we were told that buses would be there shortly to take us to our staging area. We all noticed pallets of bottled water on the tarmac and were encouraged to take some. Remembering our briefing in Germany and the literature given us about surviving in the desert, we all began to drink water. It had been a long, hot ride in the C-141 and we were all thirsty. Shortly thereafter the buses arrived.

These were old school buses you might have seen in American cities 20 years ago. There was no air conditioning, bathrooms, or comfortable seats. Before we boarded I overheard the Platoon Sergeants talking that the bus drivers were from Pakistan and didn't speak English. They had been told that the drivers knew where to go and not to worry. I put my duffel bags into the bus and found that the only seat left was directly over the wheel well. After a while most of us, myself included, were trying to rest. The bumping of the bus made me feel uncomfortable and the longer we trekked over the desert the more I needed to relieve myself of that water I had drank at the airport. I kept thinking to myself that I could hold it for a while. I reasoned that we would be there soon.

Soldiers talking a little louder awakened me some time later. Someone made the comment that he thought the drivers didn't know where they were going. They seemed to be snaking through dusty side roads instead of driving on the main road. Another made the comment that he needed to take a leak soon or he would burst. Several others agreed with him. I raised myself on one elbow enough to see the driver listening to Platoon Sergeant Montgomery, the Mortar Platoon Sergeant, with a quizzical look on his face. The more the Platoon Sergeant talked, the louder and more animated he became. I sat up quickly when the

Platoon Sergeant began shouting at the bus driver. Suddenly I could feel the tightness in my bladder and quietly prayed to God that the bus driver would stop the bus for a rest stop. Finally, the bus driver began talking on his radio to the other bus drivers.

While this was going on some soldiers were unbuttoning their pants and filling their empty water bottles with urine. One guy hadn't brought any water bottles with him. Requests to other soldiers to let him use their water bottles were met with remarks like "mines still full, I don't have any", etc. Groans and sounds of shock came from his direction as he urinated into his canteen. One guy filled his water bottle, pinched his manhood with one hand while he dumped the full bottle out of the window with the other, and then began to fill the empty bottle again. Tears were welling in my eyes as I fought back the urge to urinate. I had two full bottles of water. As I began to take the top off of one of the bottles to pour it out, the bus began to slow down and pull over to the side of the road.

I was soon in the middle of the fastest disgorging of a bus I have ever seen. It was a stampede! Someone opened the rear emergency door and the last third of the bus emptied through it. The other two thirds emptied out the front door, some cursing the driver as they went. As I stood by the side of the road slightly shaking, prickles of sweat on my back, neck and forehead I glanced to my left to see busloads of soldiers all by the side of the road relieving themselves. After the pressure in my bladder had been sufficiently relieved, I was able to chuckle to myself at the scene I was viewing. I wondered if this part of the desert had ever been watered so liberally.

3

Al Kobar Towers

The rest of the trip was uneventful. We arrived at our destination just before sunrise. To our amazement we were going to be staying in apartment buildings instead of tents! We felt so lucky and wondered how this came about. One of the officers told us that this area had more than apartment buildings; it was a whole city. The Saudi's had decided that since they had wealth from oil sales that they would be generous and build accommodations for their Arab brothers who wandered the desert, the Bedouins. Once it had been built they went to the Bedouins and told them the city was theirs. The Bedouins looked at the leadership of Saudi Arabia with disbelief and quickly declined the offer. The Saudi Arabian leaders could not understand. The Bedouins told them that for thousands of years their people had wandered the desert. All of that time they had ruled themselves. Even though it would be nice for them to inhabit a nice city like the one they had made for them, they knew that they would no longer be in control of their own lives. Their freedom was more important to them than having a nice place to live, no matter how wonderful the leadership would be. So when we arrived, the city of Al Kobar towers was empty and waiting for us.

There were concrete partitions around the edge of the city, staggered at the entrance to slow traffic to a crawl. There were triple strands of concertina (razor embedded) wire along the perimeter and a guard shack at each gate monitored by two guards. It seemed adequate enough since we were in a seemingly friendly country. There was a road next to the buildings, which ran around the outside perimeter, and immediately adjacent to this were the concrete barriers and the wire.

After sitting on our duffel bags for what seemed like a couple hours waiting to be told where we would be housed, we were shown our new accommodations. Here were apartment buildings, four stories high, which surrounded open grassy areas. On one side of the open area was a two-story parking garage with a picnic area on top. Further in the distance were a children's playground, an empty shopping center, and a huge water tower. The apartment buildings seemed to stretch for about twenty blocks long by six blocks wide. Inside the buildings were commercial carpeting, electricity and running water. The apartments were similar to many I had seen in America with a small kitchen, a living room, and several bedrooms all with white walls and blue-green carpeting. There was even a sliding glass door that opened onto a balcony.

The bathroom, however, had new rules. Since the Arabs didn't believe in toilet paper, there was no toilet paper holder. There was, however, a long metal hose attached to the cold water outlet on the toilet with a toggle switch on the end. This was how the Arabs cleaned their backsides. Since their toilets weren't made to accept toilet paper, we were told we had to place our used toilet paper in a trashcan next to it when we were done. Toilet paper would stop up the drains. I never used the hose. I could never get used to the idea of putting forced cold water on my backside then letting it air dry. However, the other way had its drawback, too. We quickly learned that the trashcan dedicated to used toilet paper needed to be taken out more than once a day, regardless if it was full or not. The first few days someone would walk into the bathroom and quickly exit yelling some expletives, extolling the rest of us to empty the trashcan when it began to stink. After this it was emptied right before first formation and every couple of hours thereafter.

We each chose a spot to sleep and set up our sleeping bags, putting down our sleeping mats on the carpet, and then forming our sleeping bags into the shape of a canoe to allow them to air out during the day. The windows were taped with masking tape in large X's in case the windows were shattered to keep them from breaking apart into thousands of shards of glass. No one was permitted to sleep near the sliding glass doors. This area would be used for assembling maps, teaching classes and meetings in general.

Even though we were short a few map panels, it was decided to tape our maps together so that we could easily continue from map panel to map panel without missing a beat. We trimmed the sides of each panel that would be attached to the other maps and left the edges on the outside maps that had map information. It became apparent early on that this was not a workable solution. We had been given over thirty maps. We were used to using no more than three at a time. Our map cases, which were used to protect the maps from the weather, could not hold all of these maps. I put together the maps I would need according to Lt. Wynn and put the rest in a plastic bag and placed it inside my duffel bag. We rarely glanced at them again.

We Bradley commanders each gave our crews lessons from the pamphlets we were given before deployment on local customs, do and don'ts, dangerous insects, etc. We were told that the Saudi's would serve the morning and evening meals in the lower level of the nearest parking garage. Lunch would be an MRE (Meal, Ready to Eat). We were briefed that we had to carry our war use chemical suit, sealed at the factory in a bag, with us at all times and let our chain of command know where we were 24 hours a day. When it was time for the evening meal we all walked over to the parking garage and got in line on the entrance ramp. We all felt awkward having to carry around the clumsy chemical suit bags and swore we would find a way to put a strap on them. We noticed that a few soldiers were carrying theirs in their rucksacks or CVC (Combat Vehicle Crewmen) bags. These bags are usually used for carrying CVC helmets, gloves and other items we needed to get to quickly while we were riding in the Bradley. We decided these were good ideas. As we got to the bottom of the ramp the line broke into two lines, each winding in front of rows of tables covered with white tablecloths. Behind each table were several Saudi men dressed in white robes and headdresses. Some wore fashionable eyeglasses and gold watches. A couple of them wore simple gold rings and necklaces. Most of them seemed to be smiling and glad to be there.

The food was good, but a little different than we were used to having. There was steamed chicken in some kind of sauce, steamed carrots, some kind of round, flat bread and boxes of milk, juice, and bottled water. For desert we could take a small cake wrapped in foil with some Arabic writing on the front. These cakes were basically white cake with fruit filling in the middle. I had finished last, walking a little behind the others, as we passed a Christmas service being held in the grassy area among the buildings. Yes, it is Christmas Eve, isn't it? I thought to myself. I had forgotten it with all that had happened in the last few days. As we climbed the stairs I noticed a flyer on the door that told about a candlelight service to be held in the parking garage by our Chaplain. It was to start in about an hour so I checked to see if anyone else wanted to go and sat down to write a letter home.

I signed out on the board about 10 minutes before the start of the service. As I walked in the approaching darkness toward the parking garage I checked my back route to familiarize myself with how our building looked in the dark. As I arrived at the bottom of the ramp I was greeted by a soldier who handed me a small, unlit candle with a piece of foil around the bottom to catch the hot wax. There were about forty chairs set up with a small isle down the middle. At the front was the Chaplain behind a folding table covered with a white tablecloth. The chaplain had a religious cloth hung around his neck. On the table before him was an open Bible, a large candle on a gold candlestick, and a communion set. On each chair was a small pamphlet spelling out the order of the short service with the drawing of a lit candle on the cover. The candle on the table was casting the only light in the area.

The Christmas story was retold, a prayer was offered and communion was given. After communion was received, we stood up and the Chaplain lit his candle from the large one on the table. He said a few words about the light going throughout the world and asked each person to light their candle from the person next to them. He then lit the candle of the first person in the first row and people then lit theirs in secession off of this candle. As the number of flames began to grow like small twinkling stars they illuminated the faces of those who held them. The feeling that this was truly a special moment began to grow. The Chaplain asked us to sing Silent Night as we exited the area starting with the first row, with each row leaving in secession. It seemed surreal as I walked through the darkness in a line of soldiers holding candles softly singing Silent Night. The beautiful sound softly echoed inside the empty parking garage. The hollowness of the open concrete building gave fullness to our voices I had never heard before. As the song ended we continued to walk to our separate buildings with our candles lit. As I reached my building I approached the illuminated stairwell and reluctantly snuffed out my candle. I felt as if I was floating, my boots barely touching the stairs. I walked over to the board and erased my name, then went to my sleeping bag and crawled inside. I fell asleep immediately and slept more soundly than I had in months.

The next morning we woke to a beautiful day. Most of these days spent at Kobar towers had wonderful weather. We were given the day off and most of us wrote letters and lounged around in our sleeping bags. In the afternoon I went for a walk to see what the area looked like. I could see a building that looked like a shopping center. I was curious to see if there was anything there unique to

Saudi Arabia. There was also a place on top of our parking garage that had a covered picnic table. It looked like a cool place to sit and think or enjoy a lunch.

As I walked into the courtyard I had to take note of our situation. Sure, we had no furniture, no transportation into town and we were restricted to this area but we were living in an apartment building! It wasn't like the cavalry to have such luck. Usually we would be housed in a tent or old barracks. As I walked toward the shopping center I could tell from a distance that it was not open. There were no soldiers walking toward this large one story building. As I walked closer I could tell the lights were not on. I was curious to see if there was anything inside. The building was empty except for a few boxes on the floor. The rest of the area was just more apartment buildings. I looked toward the mushroom shaped water tower. It was huge, sitting in the middle of this large complex. It was the tallest thing I saw in the Middle East except for the space needle in Kuwait City. At the halfway point near the water tower triple strands of concertina wire had been strung across from one side of the complex to the other. Apparently they didn't want us going into that part of the complex. I could see more parking garages and another shopping center in the other half of the complex that seemed totally empty.

I walked over to the parking garage and up the steps to the roof. The picnic area was indeed shaded, but it was still a little hotter than I expected. There wasn't much wind because the apartments blocked it and the asphalt roof reflected the heat of the sun. It was a nice view though. I could see a children's' playground behind the parking garage I hadn't noticed from the apartments balcony. It seemed so lifeless without children playing. For a brief second I imagined how wonderful it would be to see children playing on the playground. I knew it would give everyone a lift to see such innocence in this troubled land. I wondered when I would ever see children playing again. I could almost here the laughter of children reverberating off the walls of the apartment compound. I shook my head to bring me back to reality. There was no point to thinking like this, I told myself. I needed to focus on what we needed to do to get ready. Were we as prepared as we needed to be? What did I still need to know? What exactly was our mission? When would our Bradleys arrive? Was there anything we had forgotten? Exactly how safe was it where we were staying?

I decided I wanted to see more of the layout of this complex. I also had some questions to ask the leadership and my men. I walked back to the apartment building and shuffled up the stairs. Just as I was walking inside the apartment several of the men were getting ready to go to the roof to take a look around. I was about to ask if we had permission to do so, but noticed someone senior to me taking the lead in this endeavor and gladly joined in on the fun. We climbed some metal stairs to an open roof hatch and stepped onto the asphalt roof. There was a small wall around the edge about waist high which helped calm my vertigo. I walked over to the south side and looked over the edge of the wall. Below we could see more troops arriving. There were cattle trucks filled with duffel bags, buses parked next to the buildings and soldiers sprawled out on the grass just as we had done. I could see the concrete barriers with the concertina wire surrounding the perimeter. I knew this wouldn't stop much. A man could step on the concertina wire and cross over the barrier in a matter of seconds. But there was only one road into the compound and it was guarded. The only other way to get around the barriers was to cross the desert on foot. Few men would be courageous enough for that.

Little could be seen between the buildings, but on the other side I could see the layout of the place much better. I could now see the playground, the parking garage and how several buildings surrounded a small section of grass. There were many of these areas that had three buildings on the north and south, two buildings on the west and a parking garage on the east with a playground further on. I wondered how many people could be housed in such a place.

We climbed back down and went to the apartment. We lounged around some more and then the postal clerk came in with a bag of "any service member" mail. This was mail written to anyone from someone in the States who wanted to let us know they supported us. The first day no one took any. By the third day, after it had been put out that we might not be getting regular mail for weeks, almost everyone took at least one. I carefully read the ones I took. Sure, they were encouraging. But they were generic. The people who wrote them didn't know us from Methuselah. But at least we had something to read from Americans. We wondered if we would be supported by the American people after the war or be spit upon when we returned. It was good to know that at least there were patriotic Americans who cared enough to write us. I wrote each one a short note thanking them for writing us. Only one ever wrote me a second time. After the third letter even this person stopped writing. It was just so impersonal. There was only so much we could talk about with someone we had never met.

We kept asking about the mail in a vain attempt to give us some hope that we would get a letter from someone we knew. At some point we just stopped asking. How could the military postal service ever hope to find and deliver mail from points all over the globe to almost a half million military personnel who had no permanent address in a matter of days? We were asking too much. The loneliness of this time was crushing. Even though we were surrounded by men in our platoon, we had no social life. We had no mail; we had no escape from the boredom of this place. We passed our days running and doing physical training in the morning to adapt ourselves to the desert and keep in good shape. We practiced living in full chemical protective gear to get used to the experience of living in a chemical environment. We gave classes in desert survival, dangerous insects, and NBC (nuclear, biological, and chemical) warfare. We gave classes on platoon tactics, Islamic customs and beliefs, and map reading. There were even more classes on target recognition, load plans, and land mines. It got to a point where we would repeat classes and have the privates give the class. We would have games to see which section knew the most on different subjects. We were frankly getting tired of classes.

One morning a curious thing happened. Those of us with pistols were told to draw seven rounds from the arms room. I wondered why we would be getting these rounds. Never before had we been issued rounds without immediately going on guard duty or to the firing range. It felt strange. Now I had the added concern of keeping my loaded pistol secure even when I slept. The first night I tried sleeping with my holster strapped to my shoulder. It was very uncomfortable and gave me a bruise on my ribcage. Each night after that I would stuff my pistol into the bottom of my sleeping bag in its holster. I have always been a light sleeper. I knew that if anyone tried to take it while I slept I would wake before they had a chance. Since every NCO and officer now had a loaded pistol it was unlikely anyone would try.

The next morning we went for our morning run and took showers afterward. After some more classes we were given a break. Several of us walked out onto the balcony to get some fresh air. Across the grassy open area was another apartment building facing us. I noticed what looked like steam rising from the top of this building and some people walking around on top of it. Upon closer inspection, I realized that the people were Arabs. What were Arabs doing in our compound, I wondered? Apparently these men were sealing the top of the roof with tar. It seemed curious to me to see them working inside our compound. How does anyone tell one Arab from another? How were we to know if these men were friendly or not? Does an Iraqi look different than a Saudi? As I pondered these things the men on the roof apparently took a break. They all walked over to the side of the roof and stood there looking down. Immediately I had flashbacks of the Munich Olympics. I remembered the sight of Arab men looking down from rooftops and balconies in the apartment complex at the Olympic village. I remembered the Israelis who had been terrorized and killed by these men. I remembered the fear they had caused. I had to look away.

Maybe this was the reason we had been issued ammunition. As these men casually walked away and began to work I felt foolish. Surely these men meant us no harm. They were just doing their job like everyone else. It was reasonable to assume that these men had been thoroughly screened before they had been allowed to work at the compound. I was being unreasonable. I felt a little calmer as I went back inside and took one last look at the men on the roof. They were thoroughly preoccupied with their work. There was nothing to worry about.

I was asked to go to the apartment building where headquarters was located and get an easel with butcher paper on it so we could have visual props for our lessons. On the way up the stairs I noticed that the supply sergeant had a TV set turned on to CNN. I hadn't seen TV since we left Germany so I watched it as I waited on someone to get me the easel. It was like a window on the world. We didn't even know what was happening. We were out of touch. I wondered how we could even get a signal.

After I learned of this TV I would sneak over to the supply room in the evenings and listen to the TV for a few minutes. Even a little news was like water to a thirsty man. We were cut off for the most part from news of the world. Sure, we got a briefing through channels from time to time about some things that had happened. But it just wasn't enough. I learned that the nation was supporting us and patriotism was high. I learned of the diplomacy going on to try and avert war. I learned that life was going on as usual in much of the world.

One day, I noticed that speakers were being installed at several places inside the compound. It was told to us in a briefing that these were for announcements over a PA system for everyone in the compound. Sirens were also being installed which would alert us if we were being attacked. I knew at that point that we weren't in Kansas any more. Things were starting to get serious. One long blast would indicate an incoming missile. Two short blasts would indicate the all clear. We were told that there would be a test one evening so that we could practice what we needed to do. There would be periodic random tests thereafter to keep us on our toes.

The first test was nerve racking since we knew it would be coming. Our practice NBC suits were all laid out so we could climb into them easily. Our rubber NBC booties that we tied on over our leather boots were placed open, at the foot of our NBC suits. The black rubber gloves with white cotton inserts were placed within easy reach. Most of us had our protective masks out of the carriers ready to be worn. Sergeant Z had a stop watch to time us. We only had a couple of minutes to put everything on before our gear was ineffective against an attack.

All of the windows and doors were to be closed, the air conditioner shut off and everyone moved away from the windows. These precautions would give us a little more time and protection against nuclear fallout, chemical vapor and insects full of biological agents. We made sure our canteens were full since we could be in a contaminated environment for days. Water was about the only nourishment we would have during that time. Dehydration would be one of our worst enemies.

I was writing a letter when the siren went off and the loudspeaker announced that it was only a drill. The lights went off as each of us instinctively reached for our gas masks, held our breath and closed our eyes. I fumbled for my mask since it wasn't where it normally was, strapped to my side. I had to take a peak to make sure I was holding it properly to put it on. I wasn't. I turned the mask in my hands to the proper position and closed my eye again. As I pulled the mask over my head I wondered if anyone had seen me open my eye. If we had been hit with chemicals, the vapor entering my eye for even a second could have blinded me, or worse.

I cleared my mask by covering the inlet valve with my hand and blowing out. Then I sealed the mask to my face by inhaling with my hand still over the inlet valve. I opened by eyes and began putting my chemical suit on over my clothes. It was difficult. After slipping into my pants I stood up to adjust the waistband. As I did, I had forgotten that the mask carrier was not strapped to my body as usual. The type of mask I had was one I could hook to the Bradleys chemical filter through a hose. It was made with a filter attached to a hose that ran about two feet to the mask. The filter was secured inside the mask carrier with Velcro straps. Since the carrier was not strapped to my body, when I stood up the mask pulled away from my face as the hose stretched to its maximum length and jerked me back in the direction of the floor.

Now the seal on my mask was broken and I had to tuck the carrier under one arm, clear the mask again, then seal it again. I had to put on my top while struggling to keep the mask carrier from falling to the floor. I put one arm through the armhole then shifted the carrier to the other arm while I put the other arm through. I sat down in a sweat after I had closed all the zippers and stuck my boots inside my rubber booties. Sergeant Z stuck his head in our doorway with the stopwatch in one hand and a flashlight in the other. He wanted to know what was taking us so long. Just then I finished tying my booties and pulled on the white gloves. "Almost done" I muffled through my mask, sweat streaming down my face. As I pulled my rubber gloves on and tucked them under the elastic wrist of my chemical suit I looked around to see who was finished. Only one other man was still fighting with his gloves. As soon as he was finished I yelled that we were done. Someone from another room called out after me and Sergeant Z called "time". We had beat the clock but not by much.

I looked around at my men. One man had forgotten to zip his suit all the way to the top. Another had forgotten to tuck his gloves into his sleeves and still another had the face blank of his mask full of fog, indicating that his mask was not sealed. SPC Burns pointed out that the hood on my mask was askew. I had forgotten to fasten the straps under my arms to ensure full coverage on my head. My neck was totally unprotected.

I felt foolish. We had all practiced putting on this gear many times, but never like this. I had assumed that this little task would be a breeze. We would all need to think through what we needed to do and check each other to insure that it was done properly. A few minutes later the all clear was given and we laughed about the whole situation. We knew what to do. We knew we could handle it. We just had to do better next time. The next drill was in the afternoon. Because there was daylight we could see what we were doing. We also knew the mistakes we had made previously and made attempts to not repeat them. This time things went much better and we had time to spare.

That evening no one was ready to go to early chow, so I went by myself. It felt good not to have the same people around me 24 hours a day. We all needed a break. I felt an urgent need to socialize. I got in line on the ramp leading down to the eating area. In front of me was someone shorter than I with a funky grayish plastic protective cover on their helmet. I had never seen one of these chemical protective covers before. I wondered how some units had them and our unit didn't. I could here feminine voices talking in front of me. The soldier in front of me spoke to them. It was feminine, too.

After she stopped speaking she turned around slightly and glanced up at me. I asked her how she was able to get one of those helmet covers when I had never seen one before. She replied that their unit NBC NCO had issued them to everyone in their unit before they left the US. This started a conversation that made me feel alive again. After we got our food I asked if I could sit with her and she made room for me at her table. She was with a National Guard water treatment unit. I had never heard of such a unit. These types of units were placed so far from the front lines that I had never rubbed elbows with these people my whole career.

Her name was Kathy. She was in her early twenties, single, with an innocence that made me want to protect her. She had auburn hair and light blue eyes. Her attitude, speech and body language did not give a hint of military bearing. She seemed out of place wearing military gear. After we ate we walked out together and I headed back to my apartment, waiting for her to break off at some point and head to another building. I stopped at the entrance to my building; she took another step and turned around. "Do you live in this building", she asked? "Yes", I said, "on the second floor". "Well, maybe we'll see each other from time to time", she said smiling. "That's my building", she said pointing to the building next door". "OK, I'll see you later", I said. I couldn't believe my luck. I had actually met someone on my first attempt who liked me and I liked her.

There was electricity in the air. It was New Years Eve. Everyone was in good spirits. I couldn't explain it. It felt like we were on vacation rather than preparing for war. It was hard for us to keep focused on anything. There was something magic in the air. We had made it another year and we were not at war. War with Iraq seemed almost surreal. Diplomats were still negotiating. Maybe there would be no war. Maybe we would be home again soon. Maybe all of this was unnecessary. Maybe the fact that we were there was enough to avert a war. Even I was swept away in the euphoria.

After the evening meal we all walked back to the apartment and sat around talking. As evening approached we were drawn to the balcony or the roof. I looked out over the compound from the balcony and watched the activity below. There were soldiers walking between buildings, standing on balconies and laughing around the picnic table on top of the parking garage. Others stared down at us from rooftops of the other apartment buildings. All of the Arabs had left hours earlier. It was just Americans. People on the sidewalks were talking with people on the second story balconies in excited, happy conversation. People on the upper balconies were talking with others above and below them. There was constant traffic on the stairwells as soldiers moved from floor to floor making friends and stirring up mischief.

The PA system squeaked and crackled as it came to life. A thump, thump, thump could be heard over the PA system as someone checked to confirm that it was on and if the volume was correct. The noise level of the conversations dropped a little. We were expecting some routine announcement. God forbid if they called a practice alert. It was neither. Someone announced that it was almost midnight local time and that they had something special for us. There was a brief silence then the sound of a cassette tape being started. *God Bless the USA* by Lee Greenwood began to play.

A hush came over the compound as we listened to the words. Soon many of us began singing along with the music. As our voices rose they reverberated throughout the area, echoing faintly in the background. Now everyone was singing, even those who were self conscious about their voices. The sound of those voices mingled with that of Lee Greenwood and his wonderful music was heavenly. As we sang the words "I'm proud to be an American" the volume rose dramatically. It felt like my chest would burst from pride. A feeling of absolute worship for my country washed over my being. Tears welled in my eyes and my voice faltered as I struggled to sing the rest of the song. There was no embarrassment, only immense pride in all of us. We were bonding as soldiers like I had never seen before or since. It is a moment seared into my memory. Patriotism was now as real as the air I breathed. It was a force that gave us the will and courage to accomplish our mission. It was a force that helped us laugh when we felt like crying. Few things in life are as powerful as American patriotism.

4

Air Force Rendezvous

We couldn't believe it. We had seen other soldiers coming back from the PX (Post Exchange) at the Air Force Base in Riyadh and wondered if we would get a chance to go to the PX. They arrived with gold chains, carpets, and other items stuffed in plastic bags, pulling out their treasures and displaying them for all to see their good fortune. Now it was our turn. I wanted to buy something from the Middle East that I couldn't find anywhere else. We were told that even though we were essentially going shopping, we still had to stay in full combat gear, including carrying a sealed chemical suit. We were told that the Iraqi scuds could still hit us. We pulled ourselves into the bed of a two-and-a-half-ton truck and took the long, long ride into Riyadh. I looked out the back as much as I could. I wanted to see how the Saudi's lived.

Everywhere on the roads and in parking areas there were small white cars and trucks. In the city there were one and two-story mud brick houses everywhere with TV antennae on top. Next to the antennae were large silver cylinders, which I was told held water. Exposed to the sun, there was no need for a hot water heater. Riding through the streets, I noted that the few palms trees I saw had been obviously planted. But the most shocking thing I saw was a Kentucky Fried Chicken restaurant.

I couldn't believe my eyes. I pointed it out to one of my buddies and he started to formulate how we could he could get some KFC. When we arrived at the air base, the truck slowly wound through the checkpoint, finally arriving at the PX. We had two hours before the truck was to pick us up. Some went to the main PX to buy boot polish, etc. Some went with me to some small shops next to the Main PX that sold local goods.

There were numerous woven carpets with scenes of palm trees, camels, and mosques. There were postcards with desert scenes, camels, etc. There were brass oil lamps, boxes, and camels. There were even Arab robes, male and female, including undergarments and headdress. I got a little of everything. I was so excited to be in such a different culture than I had ever experienced. I had the shop owner show me how to wear the men's headdress properly and looked at myself in the mirror in the bathroom later. I could see in this heat why they wore it. It was light on my head, cool from the shade it provided. My neck was getting sun burnt every day from the pounding heat of the sun. I wished that I could wear something like that to keep the sun off my neck.

I had a little time after my shopping was completed before the truck arrived so I went outside to see if anyone else had finished. My gunner, SGT Beets, was there eating a hamburger. I asked him where he got it and he pointed to a small booth just down the street. The burger wasn't much better than the food we were getting from the Saudi's, but at least the location was different. It felt good to be eating outdoors, on an air force base, in a foreign land. It somehow seemed safer there, more relaxed. More of the platoon began arriving at our prearranged pickup point, many loaded with gold chains and rings. They were all telling me about their bargains on jewelry. I doubted that any of them could tell the difference between 18 carrot and 24 carrot gold. I didn't see any of it that couldn't be bought at any jewelry store in the United States. I nodded politely and let them have their moment.

Even though we were only on an airbase, not in an actual Saudi Town, we all felt excited to be there. Sgt. Beets asked me to take his picture and that started everyone in the platoon taking pictures of each other. Several guys from the platoon would crowd around the guy wanting the picture taken and pose with him in his moment of glory. I wondered how silly we would look after we got home and viewed these pictures. It really didn't matter. We were having fun for the first time in days. Who knew if we would get another moment like this one?

The truck arrived and the next platoon jumped off for their romp at the PX. We grudgingly piled on and after a headcount and equipment check was taken, we moved off down the dusty streets. We were all surprisingly silent, lost in our thoughts of this day. I strained to see more out the back of the truck, but couldn't see much. The monotony of the desert and the hum of the truck quickly put us all to napping, dreaming of glory and the taste of Kentucky Fried Chicken.

5

The War Begins

January 16, 1991 the air war began and life in Al Kobar towers permanently changed. We went from being peacetime soldiers in a foreign land to soldiers who knew we would be attacking Iraq. Our adrenaline went from a passive concern to a notch higher when we learned that Sadam Hussein was not withdrawing from Kuwait. We were told to open one of our war chemical suits and have it ready once the deadline the President imposed on Iraq had passed. Most of us put them on before we went to sleep, leaving the zippers undone and everything else close by our sleeping bag. I felt safe, but I knew that I needed to get better at everything. Forgetting to check something in this environment could lead to disaster.

I fell asleep and awoke sweating a few hours later. With the windows closed and the chemical suits on it was difficult to sleep. I took a drink from my canteen and as I was putting the cap back the siren sounded. I was wide-awake in a split second. One of my men woke immediately, but the others continued to snooze. I put on my mask so fast it startled me then reached over and shook others awake. As soon as they woke they knew what the siren meant. There was no yawning, no rubbing of tired eyes. I was impressed by how fast everyone was finished and instinctively checked each other's equipment. A sense of pride for these men surged inside me. Our training had taken soldiers who were good at their job and made them great. That and a good dose of adrenaline!

Sergeant Z looked in on us with his flashlight and inspected our gear. He didn't say a word this time. Sergeant Beets turned on the portable radio to find out what was happening. Each crew had been given a pocket radio the Red Cross had donated. Of all the gifts we received during the war, this radio was the most valuable. It kept us in touch with the world, provided music, and let us feel that we weren't alone.

Riyadh was being attacked with scuds. There was no danger to us this time. We fell asleep with our gear on. Occasionally we would wake and take a drink of water, taking care to drink like we had been taught, resealing our mask when we were finished. After what seemed like an eternity the all clear was given. Those of us who were wakened by the signal shook the others awake. Sweaty faces appeared as the masks were removed. Where the mask touched the skin a red impression remained. It felt good to have the mask off and the chemical suit unzipped again. I took my boots off and aired out my feet. Others did the same. Foot odor was the smell of the day.

The alerts sounded again and again over the next several days, almost always targeted at Riyadh. The first time a scud was targeted at us was unnerving. When Sergeant Beets told us this one is for us we double checked our gear and got as small as possible. We braced for the impact and heard an explosion east of us. As we listened in horror a reporter on the radio pointed out to the whole world, including the Iraqis, exactly where the missile landed, about two miles east of Al Kobar. "What an Idiot" one of us yelled! "What is he thinking" someone else pointed out? "Is this guy working for the Iraqis," said another?

With the information the reporter had given, an Iraqi scud could be targeted at us with accuracy. We knew because one of the things a cavalry scout does is adjust artillery as a forward observer. The all clear was given and we all relaxed a little. I walked to the other end of the apartment to refill my canteen. When my canteen was about half full the siren began to sound. I continued to fill the canteen as everyone else scrambled back to their rooms. As soon as my canteen was full I sprinted toward my room. Just as I passed the sliding glass doors a huge explosion took the night sky from the blackest black to brilliant white. My shadow was the only thing I saw to my left as the whole room illuminated as if a giant searchlight on the balcony had just been switched on. I instinctively tucked my head into my shoulders and covered my face with my hands. One more step and the loudest explosion I have ever heard rocked the building. The window glass rattled and the building shuddered like a small earthquake. My first thought when I saw the explosion was that I was a goner and that I was in the worst place possible. The fact that the sliding glass door hadn't exploded into a million tiny splinters amazed me. Blinded somewhat from the brilliant light, I felt for the wall and the doorway to my room. I put on my mask and fell to my sleeping bag where I donned my booties and gloves. I found myself slightly trembling from the experience. No one else noticed. We were all in shock. "Wow, that was close", someone mumbled through their mouthpiece. No one else said a thing. What more could be said? As we listened on the radio the reporter, a different reporter, made mention that a patriot missile had knocked down the scud.

We all breathed a sigh of relief. We thanked God for the patriot missile system and their wonderful operators. I have no doubt that the patriot missile battery that knocked down that scud saved my life. The next morning inspectors found fragments of the missile on top of the building just north of us. If any of us had found the reporter that gave our location to the enemy God only knows what we would have done.

The next morning I walked over and found Kathy to see if she was all right. To my knowledge no one had been injured or killed in the attack, but I knew how it had affected me emotionally. It would most certainly affect her even more. If nothing else at least she would have someone to talk to about the attack. I knocked on the door and one of her roommates answered. I asked for Kathy and she went and got her. Kathy looked as if she hadn't slept all night. I asked her I could walk her to breakfast. "Sure", she said. She put on her gear and shuffled out the door. She seemed quiet this morning. I asked her if she was OK. "Yeah", she said. Then she started crying. She said she was scared. She tried to hide her face from me, but I could see the tears gently rolling down her face. "We are all scared", I told her. "I didn't think it would be like this", she sobbed, "I want to go home. I don't know why I joined. I never expected to get sent anywhere."

As we stood in line for breakfast I knew there was nothing more to say until we sat down. Even then I wondered what I could say. She wiped her tears and felt a little self-conscious, peeking around to see if anyone was watching as we walked over to a table. We sat in silence for a few moments. "I wish I was pregnant", she said, "then no one could force me to be here. They would send me someplace safe."

I was shocked at her candor. I tried a little humor to break the tension. "Well, I'd like to help you with that, but I'm afraid it's a little too late", I said with a smile. "Stop that", she said, pushing me away, the corner of her mouth beginning to smile. Her face got suddenly serious. "My boyfriend wouldn't like that", she said. I was shocked and bewildered. "I miss him so much. I haven't received a letter from him since I got here", she explained. I reminded her that none of us had received mail yet. It could be weeks before we received any. "My unit got mail two days ago", she said, "I got mail from everyone but him." My heart was breaking. My recent divorce made me empathize with her situation. She laid her head on her arms and silently sobbed. There was nothing I could say. I just sat silently as she wept.

6

Separated From The Platoon

The scud attacks continued but we never again had such a close call. We were so thankful that the air force was knocking out these scud launchers. If we had been in the desert we could have jumped on our Bradleys and moved to another location. At Al Kobar towers we were sitting ducks. Apparently the leadership realized our dangerous situation. Shortly thereafter we were moved to the port facilities. I never saw Kathy again.

We loaded onto buses and moved to the Dhahran port facilities. At the entrance was an arch with something written across its face in Arabic. We stacked our duffel bags in rows and each unit assigned a soldier to watch them. The rest of us were free to walk around and look at the area. There were temporary showers that had been built out of wood, canvas and 55 gallon barrels in the space between the docks. The wind from the gulf was blowing a cold stiff breeze through the showers. There would be no showers taken until the wind died down. No one was that foolish.

There were sinks built into two rows of temporary wooden tables with water pipes fastened at the top. Soldiers were in various stages of undress shaving, shampooing their hair, and performing other personal hygiene needs. The sinks didn't have pipes to carry the wastewater away. Wastewater fell on the asphalt underneath the tables and splashed on boots and sandaled feet. Occasionally a soldier would take a fire hose and wash the asphalt clean. Between the cleanings the asphalt was disgusting. There was toothpaste, facial hair, spit, and chewing gum among other things littering the area. I wondered who the genius was who decided to assemble this area without proper drainage for the sinks.

As I walked over to the showers I noticed that these were no better. Tiny pieces of soap, empty bottles of shampoo and pubic hair littered the ground near the showers. I decided to find another way to keep clean. SPC Burns walked over to me and pointed to some small shops near the entrance. He said they were selling food there and accepted dollars. That sounded great. A change of food would be nice. We walked side by side over to the area as he pointed out various other things to see.

As we approached one small shop a wonderful smell wafted over my senses. "Lets go in here", I suggested. I opened a glass door and before me was a variety of things to eat. Behind the glass food enclosure was food I couldn't identify. It all smelled good, but what would I get? The Arab man behind the counter saw my confusion, put a spoon in one item and offered me a bite. Whatever it was, it was very spicy. I don't like most spicy food and waved my hand in front of my mouth to let him know. His face brightened and his finger pointed up as if he knew exactly what I wanted. He took another spoon and dipped it into a second dish.

As I sampled it my mouth came alive. "Yes", I nodded. A big smile crossed his face as he scooped a bowlful and handed it to me. "Two dollars", he said with a thick accent. "What is this", I asked, pointing to the bowl with a questioning face? "Lamb curry", he replied. I walked outside and held the bowl under my nose. The aroma was heavenly. The wind at the port puffed at the steam rising from the bowl. I knew I had better eat the meal quickly or it would get cold.

I found a place out of the wind and crouched down. The bowl was empty much too fast but my appetite was satisfied. I threw the foam bowl away and walked over to a group from my unit. Everyone was talking about what they had seen. Some mentioned beautiful women they had seen, others noted the filthy shower area, and others mentioned the Arab buildings in the area and the food. Just then a soldier walked up to us and suggested we move back to our staging area. None of us moved. "Why", asked one of the group?

"Because the Arabs might be a little upset", he replied, nervously dancing in place. "What did you do", asked one of his friends, accusingly? "Well, you know how the bathrooms in Germany sometimes don't have any sinks or toilets, just a place to piss on the wall", he quickly asked? We all nodded. "Well, I needed to piss real bad and I couldn't find anything that looked like a bathroom except that one over there with the ceramic tile inside and out. So I went in there and pissed on the wall. Well, the call to prayer just sounded and now every Arab in the area is heading to that building with their prayer rugs", he said excitedly.

We exited the area at a fast walk, our hearts thumping like drums in our chests. I said a small prayer for our safety and looked around to see if any Arabs were following us. None were following. As soon as we arrived at the rows of duffel bags we were told to pick up our bags and follow everyone else to one of the warehouses. As we struggled with our heavy bags I glanced back toward the Arab buildings and saw three Arab men talking excitedly with each other. I wondered if I could walk faster. I passed a soldier who had set his bags down to get a better grip. Soon we were at the warehouse. I didn't give the situation another thought.

The huge warehouses were packed with soldiers. Even I would have trouble trying to pick someone out of this crowd. We sat our bags down in front of the huge door openings. We were given a briefing on our stay. Our area was taped off on the concrete floor with our unit written on the tape. A large stack of cots on one wall was for our use. We were not to leave the warehouse area except for personal hygiene. Food would be served at the opposite end of the warehouse. As usual we would draw an MRE for lunch.

We would be notified when our vehicles arrived. Once we were notified we would have thirty minutes to pack our gear and move to the designated dock. A list of ships with the vehicles on board was posted at one end of the building. I found my ship and jotted down the name. Next to the name was jotted *delayed in France*. What did it mean delayed in France? My Bradley hadn't shipped out of France. Why would it be in France? I found Sergeant Z and told him about the note next to my ships name. He said that he would find out what it meant.

I went back to the list to see if there were other ships delayed. It seemed like mine was the only one. I noticed that only my two Bradleys were on this ship. The rest of the platoons Bradleys were on another ship that hadn't been delayed. At the next briefing I was told that my ship had needed repairs so it was towed into a port in France. It was unknown when the repairs would be completed or when it would arrive.

We assembled our cots and put them in the designated space. We now had about two feet between cots. With limited space we were told to only take what we needed out of our bags and stack the duffle bags in the corner. I stuffed my rucksack with everything I needed, canoed my sleeping bag, and took a nap. I woke to the sound of a TV. Someone in our unit had connected a TV and was watching CNN. I walked over and joined the small group watching TV. There were blurbs about air attacks and some news from home. I was glad we could now get *Stars and Stripes,* a radio channel and CNN. We still hadn't received any mail. I wondered when or if my mail would ever find me.

Ships continued to arrive. Soon the ship carrying the bulk of the platoons Bradleys arrived. Sergeant Z told me to just find them as soon as I could after my Bradleys arrived. After the cots were folded and stacked against the wall the place seemed empty. Now it was just my two crews and a few others from the unit. We were told to move to another area of the building to make room for more soldiers. At least the TV was still there. I watched it even more now.

Jan. 29, 1991 I was walking by the TV when a news alert flashed across the screen. Iraqi armored units were moving south into Saudi Arabia toward Khafji. I got closer to see where this city was on the map. It was directly north of us a few miles. I felt exposed, vulnerable. Even though I knew there were units deployed between us and the Iraqi units, a determined Iraqi armored unit backed with artillery and other assets just might break through. If they did there would be little to stop them according to CNN. I looked at my pistol with seven rounds and felt totally inadequate. For the remainder of the battle, except for needed naps, I was glued to the TV. We held our breath as the air force was called to hit them. Once the battle was decided we all cheered and took a much needed long nap.

Finally, our day came. Our Bradleys would be arriving today. We were told to pack everything and go down to the dock and wait. After our Bradleys were off-loaded we were to inventory everything inside and let the command know if anything was missing. We were given a map to follow from the docks to our rendezvous point with the rest of our platoon in the desert. We had two stops to make.

The first was to a painting station where the Bradleys would be painted in desert camouflage. We would be there for a while because the Bradleys would not be returned to us until the paint was dry, which would be a few hours. Even with fast drying paint in the hot desert air, some things could not be rushed. We were given masking tape to tape over anything that was not to be painted. There were contacts for the TOW missile system that had to be covered, all lights and glass.

The main gun would not be put in until we arrived in the desert. The holes for all the guns had to be covered, too. The paint was caustic when wet and hazardous to breathe. It was designed to be chemical repellant. We would be able to return to combat much quicker. From the paint station we were to go to a loading dock close by. There we would load our Bradleys on a flatbed truck to be transported to our unit.

We felt restless as we waited for our ship to arrive. I had the name of the ship and the dock number on a piece of paper the dock foreman had given us. In the distance I saw a ship slowly moving toward our dock. I was perplexed. Surely this was not our ship. It looked more like a ferry than an ocean going ship. I walked back over to my duffel bags and sat down on them. As the ship came nearer I looked to see if I could read the name. There it was; it was our ship! I couldn't believe it. I erroneously thought that the ship would be like many I had seen that were over a football field long with huge cranes hanging from the center. Here was a ship less than half that size with two upper decks that had white painted railings. The lower part of the ship was painted a very dark blue green color. All over the ship I saw flecks of rust and peeling paint. I understood now why the ship had broken down. It was obvious this ship hadn't been in dry dock in years. It was well overdue for a close look at maintenance. As the ship neared the dock it pulled to a concrete ramp. I was surprised to see how quickly they docked and lowered the ships ramp. As I looked to find my Bradleys I was delighted to find that they were right in front, the first vehicles to come off the ship. What luck; now we could get moving.

Our drivers drove our Bradleys off the ship and parked them near the gate. My men took a look inside the vehicles to see if anything was missing or damaged while I checked the outside of the Bradleys. Both crews indicated that the locks had been broken and the items we had stored inside had been stolen. All of the books we were going to read, toilet paper, candy, paper towels, and a variety of other things we had packed to make life in the desert a little more bearable were gone. The French dockworkers had stolen it all. Thankfully, all the essentials had been sent in locked Conexes on another ship. The dock master matched the shipping roster to the paper they had given me. I signed his book and my crews loaded onto our Bradleys. We followed our instructions to the painting station. As we moved I felt betrayed by the French. They were supposed to be our allies. How could they steal from soldiers going to live in the desert? I put it out of my mind and was grateful they hadn't damaged the Bradleys.

We arrived at the painting station and stopped some distance away at a sign that instructed us to wait until told to move forward. While we waited we taped all the items that needed to be taped and double-checked that we had not missed taping anything. There was only one vehicle in front of us. Just as it was pulling away from the station my two crews finished the taping. The painting station was nothing more than a tent with the two side flaps down. The rest of the tent flaps had been rolled and tied out of the way. Next to the tent was a truck with a large tank and a portable generator. Two men dressed head to toe in disposable painter's clothes wearing goggles and a breathing apparatus waved large paint sprayers attached to long thick hoses. As soon as the first Bradley was painted the painters waved for the driver to come and drive it away. Then the next Bradley pulled forward and repeated the process. The wait seemed like it lasted forever. We ate lunch and wished we had those books to read the French had stolen. We all took a short nap. After a few hours we were told the Bradleys were ready; the paint was dry.

I could still faintly smell the fresh paint. Our Bradleys now looked different. We double-checked that we had the right ones. Our bumper numbers, which identified our unit and vehicle number, were gone. Sergeant Z had stencils to mark them when we arrived in the desert. It felt good that our vehicles now blended with the color of the desert. I wondered when our uniforms would do the same. When would we be getting the desert camouflage uniforms?

We climbed back on the Bradleys and moved toward the truck loading dock. By the time we arrived at the loading dock the sun was going down. We put our Bradleys in line and I went to see what was happening. I was told it would be a couple of hours before there were enough trucks to load us. There was a meal tent set up and they were serving a hot evening meal. I went back and told my section the news. There was to be a briefing by an officer in one hour about our movement to our unit in the desert. The crews rotated their turn through the chow tent so that there was always one man on the Bradleys.

When I finished eating I noticed there was still a few minutes until the briefing began. I walked over to the loading dock to see what I could find. As I did an old civilian flatbed truck backed into the loading doc. I wondered what type of vehicle they would be putting on this little truck. The military trucks that transported combat vehicles were huge beasts with large metal low-slung trailers that had ramps that folded down. I was shocked when I saw a Bradley pull onto the loading dock. Surely they were not going to put a Bradley on the back of this little truck with a wooden flatbed! The bed didn't even look wide enough.

As I watched in disbelief a nervous driver and his Bradley commander slowly, carefully loaded the Bradley onto the truck. As the Bradley moved onto the truck the flatbed creaked, groaned, squeaked, and moved like it had never had something so heavy on its back. Once loaded the track of the Bradley hung over the sides of the flatbed by about three inches on each side. The loaded truck looked very top heavy and awkward. In every instance when I had seen a vehicle loaded for transport in the Army a set of chains front and back had been crisscrossed from the vehicle to the transport vehicle for stabilization and security. Then a piece of wood called a chock block had been inserted and nailed under each of the vehicles' wheels. These people were only using chock blocks. If there was ever a time when the chains were needed, this was it. I doubted the roads and trails we would be traveling would be as good as those in Germany or the United States. A sharp turn taken too quickly or a pothole making the truck bounce could make the truck unstable and loose control. It would be easy for the Bradley to fall off the truck.

At the briefing in the failing light the officer told us about the route. There would be a rest stop about halfway where we could get hot soup, coffee and water. The trucks had no radios; if there were problems we were to just waive down the next vehicle and they would tell the person in charge of the rest stop. There was a phone there that could contact help. The trucks had room for only two passengers; the Bradley commanders and their drivers would ride with the trucks. All others would ride on a bus.

The truck drivers were contract drivers from Pakistan. They spoke little or no English. The officer paused and asked us to move in a little closer. His voice dropped a few decibels as he told us this next part. He stated that these drivers didn't make much money. There were rumors that these drivers had been offered $3,000 for each soldier they killed and even more money if they drove their trucks across the border into Iraq with their cargo intact. The road we were to travel was only about thirty miles south of the Iraqi border.

My breathing stopped. I heard a few gasps; then a low murmur ran through the assembled group. I was horrified. It seemed like everything about this trip was as risky as the war itself. The officer then told us that there would be no convoy per se. We would move in groups, but none of the truck drivers were directed to stay in this group once it began. Some trucks were faster than others and would be allowed to pass slower trucks. It would be possible for slower trucks to be strung out for miles.

Additionally, there was no security for these trucks. No one would be watching these vehicles from a helicopter or even a gun jeep. If one of the trucks headed for Iraq it could be days before anyone would know. "Are there any questions", asked the officer? I had one. Someone beat me to it. "Where are the tie-down chains", he asked? "There are none; next question", was the reply. "Is there any good news" came a voice from the back of the group? We all chuckled and laughed nervously at first, then relaxed as we realized the confidence of camaraderie.

"Not today", came the reply. The officer looked around at the now silent group and dismissed us. The map route instructed us to follow a road that ran north for several miles then due west. The road then ran near an oil pipeline to a point in the desert where the road just ran out. This was Tap line road, later known as MSR (main supply route) Dodge. From there we would follow trails west and south to a point where the Bradleys would be offloaded. There we would be reunited with our platoon.

7

Money On My Head

My Bradleys were almost loaded when I got to the dock. As soon as they were loaded I briefed my men on what I knew. The gunners and dismounts reluctantly grabbed some personal items and headed to the bus. I drew my pistol, chambered a round and returned it to my holster. My driver, Chamberlain, and I walked over to the truck that had our Bradley. A small, thin little man stood by the truck brewing some Arab coffee on the fender. There was a small gas fueled one-burner cooking stove just big enough to hold a small three-cup teapot. He had dark olive skin, sunken eyes and a ready grin. As he smiled I noticed his broken front tooth. He nodded politely and gestured as if to ask if I wanted any coffee. I politely declined. I had heard about Arab coffee. It was strong enough to peel paint. And after what I had heard at the briefing, I wasn't about to trust anything this man would offer me.

We climbed on board as the truck driver put away his stove. I told chamberlain that I wanted the place by the door and asked him to get in first. I wanted to be able to get out quickly if needed and have some space between the truck driver and me. Chamberlain didn't mind. We climbed in and put our gear on the floor. I kept my helmet and holster. I made sure Chamberlains M16 was tucked between the door and me. We were soon moving. The truck driver smiled at me and revved the engine to indicate that he thought his truck was faster than the other trucks. I hoped he was right. I didn't want this truck to lag to the end of the group.

I looked around the cab of the truck. There was a fabric edging which had been glued around the edge of the front window that had fussy little cloth balls hanging down. We had always referred to this edging as dingle-balls. I had to break a little smile. Surely this driver was not the horrible person I imagined if he had something so decorative around his windshield. Still, there was much to loose if I was wrong. I didn't want to take that chance.

I knew I would have to stay awake all night. I knew Chamberlain didn't have the same concerns as I and would have a hard time staying awake. I couldn't risk waking up inside Iraq, if I woke at all. As we bounced along gently on the asphalt road I looked at the face of this man who was partially lit by the dashboard. He looked gentle enough, but then a lot of bad men look that way. Not all bad-men look like Charles Manson.

The hum of the road was monotonous. Chamberlain had found a comfortable way to sleep. We soldiers could sleep about anywhere. I remember a day in Germany when we awoke in the middle of the night to draw weapons and ride in a truck to a live-fire range. When we arrived the trucks left for another mission. We were all still very tired, having had our sleep interrupted. However, the range had not opened and there was no place for us to wait. We all grabbed a place to rest and tried to get comfortable. After I woke a while later I found the group sleeping in every imaginable place. There were soldiers propped against trees, in ditches, against walls and even in the gutters. Standing there watching them motionless on the ground it looked at first glance like an artillery round had exploded and scattered them. I secretly hoped I would never see such a scene for real.

My head bobbed and I realized I had dozed off. I shook my head and rubbed my eyes. I looked over at the driver who was smiling at me. What was he thinking? Was he gleeful that I had dozed off? Was he waiting for me to go to sleep so that he could make his move? Or was he just thinking that I should have taken his offer of coffee so that I could stay awake. It didn't matter. I was a little more determined to stay awake now.

The monotone sound of the engine droned on. I noticed that there was now a gap between us and the truck directly to our front. I could no longer see the bus that was farther ahead. One of the trucks now slowly began to pass us. As the truck passed us on the left I hoped there wasn't a truck coming back the other way with its headlights off. Its driver waved to my driver as if to remind him that he had the faster truck. It wasn't so much that his truck was more powerful; he was carrying a much lighter vehicle. I closed my eyes for a few minutes, making sure I stayed awake enough to hear what was happening. I kept my hand on my pistol during these short catnaps with my pistol hold-down strap unbuttoned and my thumb ready to flip the safety if needed.

There had been many times during my Army career when I had to perfect this technique. At times during nighttime guard duty, CQ (Charge of Quarters), and other nighttime duties your body craves sleep as much as oxygen. When denied sleep there are only three options. A person can fall into a deep sleep that will jeopardize the mission, sleep for a few minutes and have someone wake you, or teach yourself to fall into a semi trance. This last option was not one that some-one taught me. It was learned out of necessity. The first option was one I never considered. The second option was one I would use occasionally if I trusted a per-son who was on duty with me. But many, many times there was just no one, trusted or otherwise, available. I taught myself to do this. I could hear everything going on around me and could wake myself in an instant if needed. After a few minutes, if I hadn't heard anything, I would wake myself anyway and take a look around. I knew a guy in High School who could do the same thing. He would lay his head on the desk while the teacher was talking. Once the teacher had noticed what he was doing, the teacher would call this to everyone's attention and ask the guy a question on what had just been said. The guy would raise his head and repeat word for word what the teacher had said to everyone's amazement.

Another truck passed us and its taillights got smaller and smaller in the dis-tance. Then another passed. I began to get concerned. At a slight curve in the road I looked into the rear view mirror to see how many vehicles were behind us. There were still four sets of headlights. How many of these would pass us before we reached our destination? Suddenly the asphalt road was gone. Now we were on a desert road similar to the one we had just left, but without the asphalt. There was still a ditch on each side. It was still two lanes wide. It was flat and nicely graded. But now there was dust. I was glad that the truck to our front was far enough ahead that we weren't eating its dust.

The truck hit a bump and jolted my eyes open. The driver was smiling again. He motioned down the road, nodding his head as he did. In the distance I could see a faint light coming from a building. We must be at the midway point, I thought. As we neared the building I could see several trucks parked along the road. Our driver pulled over and parked behind the short line of trucks and motioned us to get out. Chamberlain was now awake and we got out to stretch our legs. I asked Chamberlain if he was going to get some soup. He rubbed his eyes and said yes. I told him I wanted to keep an eye on the truck and he offered to get me some soup.

My watch read about 2 AM. I yawned, stretched my arms and legs, and walked around our truck. Our driver smiled at me as I walked around to where he was brewing coffee on the fender of the truck again. He offered me some coffee in the same way he did at the beginning of this trip. Again I declined. I wondered where Chamberlain was with the soup. It was a little chilly and I rubbed my hands together to get them warm. Our driver smiled again as he emphasized the fact that his hands were wrapped around a hot cup of coffee. I waived him off and walked around the truck marveling that the Bradley was still sitting on it. I had to admit that we hadn't had any problems so far.

I noticed one of the other trucks had a flat tire. Four drivers were looking at the flat tire discussing how to jack the truck in this sand with so much weight on it. I scrutinized the tires on our truck. The tread was a little deficient but the tires looked good otherwise. I nodded to our driver and motioned toward the scene. He smiled, kicked the tire next to him and gave me the thumbs up. I felt a little better. I just hoped he wasn't pulling my leg.

Chamberlain arrived with a Styrofoam cup full of chicken noodle soup. He said there was quite a line inside the building. Heat rose in waves from the top of the soup. I felt a shiver go up my back. Chamberlain and I got in the truck to eat the soup. I knew the soup wouldn't help keep me awake. It would have the opposite effect. I kicked myself for not getting coffee instead. I ate a few spoonfuls and sipped some of the hot liquid then walked over to a fifty-five-gallon barrel and placed the cup inside. The lead trucks had already pulled out. Others were warming their engines or moving slowly back onto the road. I walked back to my truck. The driver was storing his coffeepot and stove. The stove was placed in a thick hot pad made to fit it. The heat had scorched the fabric.

As we pulled out I felt good that things had gone well so far. The engine lapsed into a monotonous hum. The headlights illuminated a bland desert scene. Chamberlain was snoring lightly. The soup warmed my insides. The trucks' heater was working well. The conspiracy was complete. The light trance didn't last long. I was in dream world.

A jolt shook me awake. My hand had shaken loose from my pistol and dropped to my lap. I immediately grabbed it again and looked around to see the situation. The truck had hit a pothole. The driver seemed unconcerned. I felt the bed of the truck rock slightly, heard the springs creak. We were still in the line of trucks. Unless all of them were headed for Iraq, everything was OK. I rolled down the window and looked up at the stars. My compass didn't work correctly inside the metal truck so I located the Big Dipper and found the North Star. We were still headed west. The road was getting worse. There were no more ditches, only a trail that had been leveled. Instead of the nice wide road we now had barely enough room to pass anyone. From time to time a pothole would be seen. Our driver seemed to be concentrating more on the road and was moving slower than we had on the good road. The night rolled on endlessly.

I wondered if we would be allowed to sleep when we got to our unit. After what seemed like an eternity, the line of trucks finally turned south. It seemed like we were a million miles from nowhere. I hadn't seen a tree, a telephone pole, or an electric line the whole trip. They must have buried the phone and electric lines to the rest stop, I reasoned. I began to notice that the sky was getting a little lighter. Instead of blackness dotted with stars there was a dark blue sky with a lighter blue as it approached the eastern horizon. It was beginning to dawn a new day. I snapped the hold down strap on my holster and rested my eyes for a while. The next time I opened my eyes it was even lighter outside. I sat up straight and stretched my arms and legs, trying hard not to waken Chamberlain. My throat felt as dry as cotton. I cleared my throat, trying to muffle the sound and took a swig of water from my canteen. Ahead of us trucks were turning off the road into an open area to the left. I could see there were two unloading ramps made of concrete. We had arrived. The long trip was over.

8

The Middle Of Nowhere

The sun was just breaking the horizon as we waited for our chance to unload. I woke Chamberlain so he would be alert when it was our turn. We both got out and walked around to get out of our stupor while the truck got set at the ramp. Once the truck was set Chamberlain got in the drivers' hatch and started the engine while our truck driver removed the back two chock blocks. I guided Chamberlain as he slowly backed the Bradley off the ramp. Once unloaded our truck driver smiled and waved to us then jumped into his truck and sped off the way we had just traveled.

A sense of loneliness overwhelmed me. It was just my two Bradleys now and our platoon was nowhere in sight. There was a large sign in this makeshift parking lot that told everyone to tune to a certain frequency and give a radio call when we arrived. We screwed our antennas into their bases, turned on the radio and set the radio to the requested frequency. I called in and told the radio operator I needed to find my platoon. He gave me their frequency and that of the company. He said that my platoon was on a firing range and would be out of range of my radio. He suggested calling my company and they would direct me to the platoon. Then he gave me a direction to travel and approximately how far it was to our Company area.

The soldiers who had ridden the bus had loaded onto the Bradleys while I was doing this. I waved to my other Bradley to follow us and we moved out. The voice on the radio was reassuring. We weren't alone. However, traveling in the desert without landmarks was a very different animal than traveling in Germany. The contrast was startling. The huge desert expanse made me feel as small as an ant. It would be easy to miss our unit if our direction was off even a little. I quickly found a trail heading in the general direction the radio operator had given. I hoped that it would lead to our unit.

I had Chamberlain keep an eye on the odometer and instructed him to tell me when we were one mile from the stated distance. He keyed his mike and said we had reached one mile out just as we were topping a small rise in the ground. Just beyond the rise I could see a unit assembled on the sand, huge antennas pointing skyward marking the spot. As we neared I could see a small sign displaying our unit designation. I pulled our Bradleys to the edge of the assembly area and parked them while I went in to see where we needed to go. As I walked to the Operations tent it felt good to be back with our unit. Familiar faces were a welcome site. Now our lives had meaning and purpose again. I was given directions to our platoon at the live fire range.

I briefed my section that we were headed to the live fire range and we moved out. I wondered how a live fire range could be made in this desert without the rounds hitting anything. Most ranges are built with a background terrain of some kind that will absorb the rounds or make them ricochet harmlessly. I didn't think there would be enough variation in terrain to accomplish this in this desert. As we approached the firing range I searched the vehicles to see if I could find our platoon. I spotted the four other Bradleys of our platoon. They were parked in a row with ramps down, guns pointed skyward, crews breaking open boxes of ammo.

We pulled close then stopped to ground guide the Bradleys into their positions next to the others. I saw Sergeant Z over near the ammo point and walked over to get the word on what we needed to do. I felt a little embarrassed that we had not deployed with the rest of the platoon. I knew it had not been my fault, but the Army's emphasis on teamwork and camaraderie made it feel like I had let down the platoon. Sergeant Z looked up and saw I was walking toward him. He had seen my Bradleys pull in.

"You finally made it", he said. "Yes", I began. I wanted to tell him all that had happened, but he didn't let me continue. "You need to pull your Bradleys over to the ammo point and draw ammo. Then go over to the Range Safety Officer and let him know your crews will be firing also. He will give your crews a safety briefing and add your crews to the firing roster". "OK", I replied, turning on my heel as I headed back to my section. I hadn't even reached Sergeant Z. It felt like a slap in the face that he hadn't wanted to chat for even a moment.

I asked myself what I would've done if I were under the same pressure to get the platoons Bradleys fired. Would there be time later to talk? Of course there would. First things first I told myself. I figured I would have done the same thing. My crews were talking to the rest of the platoon about our ordeal. I told them to mount up and take the Bradleys to the ammo point to load with ammo. They cut their conversations short, raised the ramps and had the Bradleys moving toward the ammo point in short order. While they did this I walked over to the Range Safety Officer and told him my crews were on the range. He told me that once my Bradley crews had loaded the ammo to find him for a safety briefing.

One thing we would need to do was change into our Nomex (fire retardant) uniforms and put on our CVC vests. I went back and verified that the ammo count was correct. Once the Bradleys were parked I told the men to change into Nomex, including the vest. It felt strange changing clothes in the open with the rest of the platoon watching. Some of the guys who were more modest, me included, went inside or between the Bradleys and changed there. SPC Allen didn't care; he just stripped on the ramp. Guys from the rest of the platoon ribbed him about liking to show off his body. They made comments like "hey, look everybody there's a strip show over there" or "whoa, look at those muscles!" and "hey Allen, I'll bet you're looking for a girlfriend, aren't you?"

SPC Allen just took it in stride and kept on changing his clothes. This was normal for the cavalry. This was one of the things guys liked about being in an all male unit. We could be ourselves and not worry about feminine sensibilities. We could be crude, even disgusting at times and nobody cared. We didn't have to put a face on for anybody. We sensed each other's insecurities, like having to undress in full view of others. But instead of being polite and just turning our heads we reveled in the fact that this was the life we chose.

In what other profession would you be made or allowed to change clothes in public? It was the price and the freedom of being a cavalry soldier. It was the feeling of being the master of everything you surveyed and the embarrassment of standing almost naked in front of fellow soldiers. It was the contrast between these two things that kept us humble. Every time we started feeling egotistical about ourselves there was always something that brought us back to earth. We felt obligated to remind each other that we weren't ten feet tall. A man with a big ego in the cavalry can get you killed.

After we were done with the firing range we returned to the base camp. The Bradleys were positioned in a semicircle facing north. The rest of the platoon had dug bunkers between their Bradleys. Now we needed to dig ours. I put Specialists Allen and Burns to work digging the bunker after drawing an outline in the sand with my boot. As this was being done Sergeant Z brought me a large black trash bag and set it on the back ramp. It was our mail that had finally found us.

The bag was full of boxes, letters and manila envelopes. My crew wanted their mail immediately. They were like hungry wolves after a rabbit. I waived them off and told them I would sort it while they finished their jobs. Chamberlain was still doing maintenance, Sergeant Beets was still cleaning weapons and Specialists Allen and Burns were still finishing the bunker. Before I was finished sorting the mail eager eyes were peering at the stacks of mail. "Are you finished with your work", I asked? "Yes", everyone said as they nodded eagerly.

I handed each a stack of mail accumulated by the Army postal service for us over the past month. I took my stack, selected five letters and put the rest back into the bag. We would be moving again soon and no one knew if the mail would follow with any regularity. From what I had seen, it wasn't likely. I would allow myself two letters a day thereafter so that I would have mail of some type from that day forward. There are few things worse than not having mail when you are stuck in a desert seven thousand miles from home.

After our positions had been finished, we had some time to ourselves. I walked a few feet away from our area and took a look around. All I could see was an endless desert. I hadn't seen any sign of life, except us, since we had left the port. The vastness of the desert made me feel small, insignificant. I wanted to pick up a phone, make contact with my family and tell them where I was living. It felt like no one in the "real world" knew where we were or even cared. The loneliness hit me like I was being smothered in a vacuum chamber.

What a change from Germany! There was not a blade of grass, a tree, or even a stream. How could anything survive in this desert? Would we survive in this desert? As I walked back to our dugout covered by a tent, it felt like even God had abandoned us. Just then, as I approached the tent, a sparrow landed on the tent rope at the entrance to our tent. I was shocked, surprised and delighted. This little bird reminded me of the song that says God looks after the sparrow, and will look after me. This little sparrow, dancing on the tent rope gave me hope and brought me out of despair. He didn't even seem afraid of me. As he flew off, I realized that even though we were in such a desolate place, God could still see us and look after us. It made me smile again.

A few days later we were told to expect rain. Rain; in this desert? I hadn't seen rain since we arrived. I figured we might get a sprinkle and didn't give it another thought. Sometime after midnight, I woke in our tent. Something was wrong. I reached for my flashlight and took a look around. As I did I could hear rain hitting the top of the tent. On one side of the tent, a small waterfall was pouring water into the bunker where we were sleeping. I looked at my sleeping bag. Water was halfway up the side. Water was beginning to seep through the sleeping bag. We had a big problem!

Someone yelled for me to stop shining the flashlight. I told him we all needed to get out of the bunker and into the Bradley. The bunker was filling with water! I started yelling for everyone to get up, shaking the ones near me. We all were shocked that this could happen in the desert. Each of us clumsily grabbed our gear and headed into the pouring rain toward the Bradley. We spent the rest of the night with the Bradley running, the heater on, trying to get dry and warm.

The next morning we surveyed the damage. I had put some of my mail under my sleeping bag so that I could read it by flashlight before I went to sleep. All of this mail was now soaked, a pile of mush on the wet bottom of the bunker. As wet as our sleeping bags were, I wondered how they would dry out before we could use them again. We threw them on top of the tent, bottom side up, with one end hanging on a tent pole. After a little more than an hour, the dry heat had thoroughly dried them out. We marveled at how quickly the desert changed. We never saw rain again while we were there. I have read since that this rain had been brought about by the Air Force seeding the clouds, forcing it to rain. Thanks a lot, guys!

Days later we were packing to move to a point just south of the Iraqi border, far west of our present position. We were already a long way into the desert. I wondered how much farther we would need to go. I remembered being home for Christmas one year, standing over a world globe showing my relatives where Germany was in relation to Kansas. We then spun the globe to the pacific and found Okinawa where my brother David had been stationed during his time in the Marine Corps. We then spun the globe back to the Middle East and found Israel since it was Christmas. I asked my Mother if she would like to go there some day. She said she didn't know. It would definitely be a long trip. I saw the vast desert east of Israel from Jordan to Iran and poked my finger at it. "Well, <u>there</u> is one place I <u>never</u> want to visit", I said with emphasis! It seemed ironic that I was now in that desert moving closer to war.

Our scout platoon would be in the lead. We began moving early in the morning before the sun rose. We moved to the start point, the same place where our Bradleys had been unloaded from the trucks, and waited for others to form a line behind us. We ate MREs for breakfast while we waited. As soon as the bulk of the units vehicles had arrived we began moving slowly, creeping so slowly that it didn't register on the speedometer. We moved west using the GPS and following a narrow desert road. A call came on the radio that we could increase speed to five miles per hour.

It still seemed like we were moving in slow motion. At that speed everything shook inside the Bradley. We could feel every track pad hit the surface. Our teeth chattered from the effect. It was like riding a jackhammer. I begged God to spur the leadership to increase our speed to ten miles per hour so we wouldn't be in such agony. Apparently God didn't speak loud enough. The agony continued. Lt. Wynn radioed that we were about to cross the wadi Al Betin, a valley made by wind and water erosion. It was the largest, most notable terrain feature we would see during our time in the Middle East.

The ground began to rise gently as we approached the valley. Looking from the top of one side of the valley to the other before we reached the crest it was difficult to see that there was a valley between. Once the crest was reached, the valley slowly opened to reveal its secret. I did a double take. It was still there. Surely the desert was playing tricks with my eyes. This desert was so cruel, I thought to myself. The more I looked at it the more I realized the scene was real. I asked Chamberlain if he saw what I saw. He raised himself and looked to the right. "I think I see a mirage", he said, "Is that real grass"? "That's what it looks like to me", I replied.

There before us was a large sod farm of many acres. Large above ground metal irrigation pipes ran the length of the farm spewing water into the air from multiple fountains. A house could be seen behind the farm near the edge of the valley in the shadows. The scene looked like it should be in California, not Saudi Arabia. The sight transfixed me. The deep green of the grass was like a magnet to my eyes. Drinking in the scene cooled my soul like a cold glass of water from the refrigerator cools a thirst. I wanted to stop and stare at the sight until I got tired of it.

But too soon, much too soon we were traveling up the other side of the valley back into the cruel, hot, merciless desert. I craned my neck to drink in the sight for as long as I could until it vanished in an instant when we crested the other side. I felt so deprived. I secretly wished I could take a square of that grass sod and mount it on the top of my Bradley. That way I could look at it as we traveled, touch it as I dismounted, and smell it before I slept. That would be a little bit of heaven. I knew it was ludicrous, but I had to have my dreams. I smiled to myself and laughed at the idea.

Once on the other side we ran out of road. Now we had to rely on our maps, but mostly the GPS and Loranz. The maps were of little value. The value of the GPS and Loranz cannot be underestimated. Without these devices, from this time to the movement into Kuwait after the war, it would have been almost impossible to move as fast or find the republican guard as easily as we did. Confusion would have been the order of the day, not the orderly movement we experienced. At a certain point indicated by the GPS my platoon turned north and spread into a linear formation.

We continued north until we reached a new reference point indicated by the GPS. My platoon formed into a semicircle and I walked over to get briefed on what we were to do. The Lt. would be going to a briefing and return with more info. We were to dig fighting positions beside our vehicles that could also be used as bunkers in case of incoming artillery. I put our dismounts, SPC Burns and SPC Allen, on this mission and they began digging. The sand was very compact at this location and difficult to dig. The crew would be challenged and get a good workout, but at least the sides wouldn't cave in. When I walked back to the Bradley Chamberlain was performing maintenance and Sergeant Beets was listening to the radio. "Any news", I asked? "Nope", came his reply.

At the evening meeting the Lt. told us that we had to send a complete report on all our systems to the maintenance teams. He handed us some blank form 2404's (maintenance request forms) and told us he needed them ASAP. I handed these out to my crews when I returned.

Sergeant Beets began inspecting the turret systems, the rest of the crew everything else. I helped Sergeant Beets with the turret system. I verified that the TOW system missile contacts extended and retracted properly, that the retractable arm locked in place and that all the safety switches engaged properly. We verified that all of the indicator lights worked and checked the humidity indicators on the turret. Once all of the checks were finished the 2404's were handed in to Sergeant Z. Mechanics would be sent to correct anything found deficient. Turret mechanics would bring their equipment to perform more checks on the turret systems.

Turret mechanics arrived the next day. They had boxes that they hooked to our turrets with several long cables and a missile tube that had been modified to check the circuitry in the launcher. When they were finished they deadlined our vehicle for a missile launcher problem. The mechanics deadlined my wingman's vehicle for a leak of some kind. Sergeant Z said that we would need to take our vehicles back to the bone yard (maintenance assembly area) to get fixed. I asked him what to do if the ground war started before we got back.

He said it shouldn't take very long to get repaired. If it took longer than expected he said to just catch up with the rest of the platoon. I smiled and said OK. I asked for a strip map to find my way since I didn't have a GPS or Loranz. He said I didn't need any, that all I needed to do was drive due south following barrels which had been placed there as reference points. When finished all I had to do was follow the barrels back to the platoon. It seemed simple enough, but I asked for and received compass directions and approximate distances anyway.

9

Lost In The Desert

We mounted the Bradleys and headed south. We followed the barrels and made good time. At one point near a small rise in the ground the trail veered slightly southwest. It was almost imperceptible. I didn't notice the change in direction at the time. It was only in retrospect that I realized what had happened. We arrived at the bone yard after traveling almost thirty miles. I announced our arrival to the mechanics and they started repairing my Bradleys almost immediately. Less than an hour and a half before sunset the mechanics announced that the vehicles were repaired.

I knew if we returned to the platoon now it would be dark well before we arrived. I called Sergeant Z on the radio but there was no answer. I couldn't reach anyone from the platoon. The headquarters tent was adjacent to the bone yard and had stronger radios than those installed on the Bradleys. I walked over to the TOC (tactical operations center) and asked to use their radio to call the platoon. The radio operator agreed and switched to our platoon frequency. I got through to the platoon but didn't get permission to stay until morning. We needed to be there at first light. We would have to leave now.

The sun was lower in the sky as I stepped out of the tent and dropping fast. We moved onto the trail and headed north. It was soon dark. It was a cloudless, moonless night but the stars were shining brightly. The heavens were a navy blue and the sand was a dark brown. We followed the barrels that were spaced about every mile. When we got to the little rise where we had veered slightly southwest there was now an intersection. Sergeant Beets was riding in his open hatch. I told the driver to go straight.

Sergeant Z had told me to follow the barrels straight back to the platoon. Sergeant Beets suggested that we should take the left fork. He remembered the little rise and the slight turn we had made. I told him my instructions but decided to verify the compass directions just in case. Clouds had now begun to move in and blanket the sky. I walked out on the road we were traveling and took a reading. The reading was within one degree of what I had been given. I walked over to the other trail and took a reading. It was three degrees off in the opposite direction. I decided to stay on the trail that went straight.

We traveled on this trail for about three miles until it began to veer to the right. I stopped the Bradleys and took another reading. Now the reading was another three degrees off. Everyone was getting impatient. They wondered why I kept stopping. Something just didn't seem right to me. I knew I was following my instructions correctly but we were now going further and further off the compass direction. I decided that we needed to move faster. I took a bearing off the North Star to give me a general direction so that I wouldn't have to keep stopping.

I had to stop the Bradley and walk some distance in front of it to get an accurate reading; otherwise the metal vehicle would disrupt the reading and make it useless. We were now moving along at a better pace. I asked Chamberlain to keep track of the mileage and call out every five miles we traveled. When he called out that we had gone fifteen miles I knew we were near the border. To our front was a unit with several tents and concertina wire strung around them. It definitely wasn't our platoon. I stopped my Bradleys several yards before an entrance, climbed down and walked over to the guard. I asked the guard his unit. He gave me a unit I had never heard before. I asked him if he knew where 4/8 Cavalry was located. He didn't know but someone in the TOC would know. He pointed to a tent with several large antennae and told me to walk over to it. I did. As I pulled back the tent flap the light blinded me. I took two steps inside and looked around. I couldn't see anyone. "Hello", I said. Someone from inside a TOC vehicle with its ramp down called to me. "Up here", he said. I stepped into the vehicle and explained my situation. "Well", he said, "you're in the wrong division. The Third Armored Division is to our left. It's a good thing you stopped here. The only thing north of us is the Iraqi border."

I studied his map and the units drawn on it. My unit was on his left with some small wadis between. I knew at night we could easily have an accident in that terrain. Also, I decided that it might not be wise to approach our tanks and Bradleys from the side. All it would take would be a misidentification and an itchy trigger finger; we would be history.

To go back to the intersection where we made the wrong turn would be a waste of time. I decided to go back behind the wadis and turn west until we reached a rear echelon unit. From there we would go north until we reached the platoon. I asked all of my men to gather around while I explained our situation. I felt like I had let the men down. I knew that they all wanted to be back with the platoon. I knew they would have questions. I had followed others around in the darkness on maneuvers in Germany and Fort Carson who seemed to be lost. I wanted to reassure the men that even though we were not where I wanted to be that I had the situation under control. I needed to win their trust.

As everyone in my section gathered around the ramp of my wingman's vehicle I studied their faces. The blue light from inside the vehicle cast a little light, enough to see that mostly the men were just tired. It had been a long day and it was going to get even longer. I laid out what had happened and told them what I knew. I then told them my plan to get back to the platoon. I asked if there were any questions. Sergeant Hall, my wingman's gunner, asked why we just didn't go straight west. I told him my reasoning. Everyone seemed to understand.

We mounted the Bradleys and turned them around. Sergeant Beets occasionally scanned the side of the road with his night sight to see when the wadis would taper off. It seemed like it took forever to find the end of them. When we could see a clear way to go west I realized I was beat. I looked at my watch. It was almost 2 AM. I needed sleep. If I was to lead these men back to the platoon by daybreak I would need a clear mind. Otherwise we could be wandering around lost for who knows how long. I made the decision to stop for an hour to recharge my energy. SGT McCullough didn't like my decision. I didn't care. I had gotten us off track by not paying attention and inaccurate information. I was not going to make it worse.

I set my watch alarm for one hour and put one of the dismounts on radio watch. Before I went to sleep I tried to reach the platoon on the radio. I could barely here their reply. It was full of static, garbled and very weak. I informed the sender of our situation. There was no reply. I signed off, hoping that someone on the other end understood.

I woke with a clear head and a tired body. We moved out as soon as the Bradleys were started and everyone was in their places. I kept the North Star on my right shoulder as we moved as quickly as possible westward in the darkness. Soon we could see large tents in the distance and steered toward them. I pulled the Bradley to the entrance of this assembly area and approached the guard. We were on the right track. This was our division; this was our aviation brigade. We only needed to go north then adjust left or right as we moved closer.

We turned north following a trail in the sand. Soon we came upon another unit and I verified that we were still on the right track. I was told that our unit was about twelve miles north of our current location. As I climbed into the commanders' hatch I asked Chamberlain to let me know when we had gone ten miles and we continued north. About an hour later he let me know we had traveled ten miles. I radioed the platoon. A weak, garbled reply was heard. My heart sank.

The signal sounded just as it had when we called from the other divisions' area. However, according to all the information I had learned we had to be close. Sergeant Beets looked around with his night sight while I looked around with my night vision goggles. We could see nothing. I knew the Iraqi border was just north of us. To move farther north without a visual sighting of our platoon position could lead us into a minefield. The terrain before us was full of small wadis.

I decided to wait at that location until daybreak, move until we found a visual on the platoon, and then move into the assembly area. I knew all of this caution seemed extreme to everyone, including me. If this had been a practice maneuver, I might have been a little more aggressive. But this was a huge desert full of the unknown. Even in practice I had seen a tank disappear into a ravine, heard of Bradleys rolling over in uneven terrain and ran into minefields in the most unlikely places. I could live with a little ribbing about being too cautious. I would have a hard time living if I lost some of my men.

Sunrise would be in about an hour and a half. I told the men to get some sleep. I set the alarm on my watch and woke to daybreak when it sounded. I called the platoon again. This time the signal sounded a little stronger and less garbled. I told the radio operator our situation and told him what I could see. He then conferred with Sergeant Z, who came on the radio and told me to find the high ground to my east. The platoon was in a valley on the other side. There was no way to the platoon but to go around the high ground to the north. To backtrack and approach from the south would take much longer. I asked him if the ground to our north was clear of mines and he yes. I asked him to let the tankers know that we were coming in from the north so they wouldn't accidentally shoot us, then made my way to the platoon assembly area.

I was beat, but I knew Sergeant Z would have questions. As soon as the Bradleys were put into position I grabbed my gear and walked over to see Sergeant Z. As soon as I saw him I started to explain. He stopped me and told me to get the men cleaned, fed and ready to move in about two hours. He was just glad I had made it with all of my men and vehicles intact. As I walked back to my Bradley I kicked myself for not noticing that the trail had veered and forked at the rise in the ground on the way to the bone yard. My only conciliation was that I had made it back in time for the day's activities with my section, tired but intact. At least that felt good.

Even though the men grumbled a little during this episode they never approached the subject again with me. What could they say? I had gone strait where I should have turned, even though my instructions had told me to go strait. Yes, I should have been more aware. But the bottom line was that we had made it intact to the platoon before the time we were needed. As I looked at my men washing their faces around the ramps of the Bradleys I felt good. These men had trusted me in a very difficult situation. I would need that trust even more when we crossed the border into Iraq. If we ran into trouble there and they were hesitant to obey my orders our safety could be in jeopardy. I felt a sense of pride in my men take shape that has lasted to this day. I shook my head in disbelief when I remembered that less than a year had passed since I sat at a desk recruiting for the Army in Cape Girardeau, Missouri. I was thankful that I had good machines, good men and the bright North Star to guide me.

10

Crossing the Iraqi border

We woke days later with the knowledge that today, February 24, 1991, we would cross the border into Iraq. At breakfast SFC Z told me I needed to go with him to a briefing from the Battalion Commander. I was a little confused. I had rarely seen the Battalion Commander since I had joined the unit. I wondered what he would want to talk to us about. We knew the mission. We knew we were ready. What else could there be to talk about? I went back to my Bradley and told my crew. They wanted to know the same thing.

I told them I didn't know but I would let them know when I got back. I grabbed my map case, checked that I had adequate paper, pens, marking pens, etc. and headed for the Platoon Leaders Bradley. SFC Z, SSG Fariello, LT Wynn and I walked on the lowered ramp and found seats in the back. As the driver raised the ramp the brightness of the desert was replaced by the darkness in the belly of the Bradley.

Arriving at the battalion TOC (Tactical Operations Center) we opened the tent flap and went inside. This was sacred ground. This was the first time I had even been invited into this TOC. Here was where all of the Battalions secrets were held, where the leadership of five companies of men held court. The hum of a portable generator would make any conversation difficult. We were invited to sit down in some gray folding chairs faced toward a large map on the far end of the tent. I expected that we would be only a portion of those receiving the briefing. Instead we were the only ones who had been invited. The portable generator switched off.

The Battalion Commander walked to the map and told us to keep our seats. He told us that, since we were the lead element, he wanted us to know more than anyone else and be clear on what he wanted. He pointed to the map and told us that the Iraqi checkpoint on the map had been taken out by an MLRS (Multiple Launch Rocket System) strike the previous evening. The engineers in several places had cut the sand berm separating Saudi Arabia from Iraq. He reminded us that we needed to move through this cut quickly, since there may be enemy artillery that hadn't been spotted zeroed in on that point.

The Second ACR (Armored Cavalry Regiment) would go over the border in front of us and lead the 7th Corps to a point about 20 miles inside Iraq. When they reached this point they would turn east to block any Iraqi units coming out of Kuwait and guard our right flank. At this point our scout platoon would be one of the lead elements of the 7th Corps. He told us that there were many mines in Iraq, mostly personnel mines. There were also many unexploded munitions on the ground, mainly cluster bombs. He recommended we not put anyone on the ground unless it was absolutely necessary.

While we were behind the 2nd ACR he told us to follow in their tracks to lesson the chance of hitting mines. He then pointed to the map and commented that according to all the intelligence information, there were no troops left from the border to the point where the 2nd ACR would turn east. They didn't know why. The experts surmised that they might have pulled their troops out so that they could hit us with chemical, biological, or even nuclear weapons. They just didn't know.

We would be covered by scout and attack helicopters. We were given their radio frequencies and call signs if we needed them for close air support. We would get an attachment of an armored NBC (Nuclear, Biological, Chemical) vehicle called a Fox. In this vehicle the crew could monitor, safely under overpressurization, to see if we had passed through any of these environments. In other words this vehicle would be immediately *behind us*. We would provide it protection from the enemy; it would provide detection awareness for the rest of the Corps. We would be on our own.

I nervously thumbed my protective mask and prayed I wouldn't need it. We were told we had priority of fires from the battalions' mortars and long-range artillery. However, since we would be on the move, it would be several minutes after we requested support before it could be provided. If we did hit a mine or break down we were to stay as close to our Bradleys as possible and as the Corps moved forward the medics and mechanics would find us. He paused and asked us if we had any questions.

My mind was reeling from the things he had said, but I had one question I needed answered. The previous day a Bradley had been attacked by one of our own helicopters, killing most of the crew. I asked the commander if anything had been done to keep this from happening again. The short answer was "no". In combat there would always be friendly fire incidents and there would probably be more. However, he smiled, the Army labs were working on systems similar to those installed on jet aircraft called IFF (Identification Friend or Foe).

These systems would not be ready for years. His only recommendations were to keep our gun barrels pointed at the enemy and display a bright orange card if we needed to go back through friendly lines. We were handed pieces of cardboard about the size of a legal envelop which had been spray painted with highway department orange paint. At night we were to continuously flash our flashlights toward friendly lines if we needed to pass. This seemed wholly inadequate, but better than nothing.

As we exited the TOC and boarded the Bradley a sense of apprehension began to grow. I was lost in my thoughts as we rumbled along back to our AA (Assembly Area). As I exited the Bradley and walked to my Bradley I could see my section anxious to here what I had learned. Their expectant eyes and casual walk toward me suggested they wanted good news, but any news would do. I took a deep breath, laid out my map on the ramp and told them what I knew. As I talked about the situation on the ground in front of us I tried not to make eye contact.

These were men, good men, wonderful human beings who in the next few days may be screaming from the pain of wounds or dead in a body bag. The briefing done, the crew silent, a grip of fear clenched my heart like a fist grasping a rubber ball. I told them that I had no idea what would happen once we crossed that berm, but I wanted them to know that they were the best men I had ever served with and felt confident in our ability to do what needed to be done. I asked if anyone objected to me reading the 23rd Psalm. Everyone shook his head no.

When I read the last word, "forever", my voice faltered and a large tear welled up in my left eye. My eyes grew misty and my body shook slightly. I walked to the front of the track to compose myself and as I did my gunner, SGT Beets, put his arm on my shoulder and, patting it slightly, softly said that it would be OK. I wiped my eyes, gave myself a body shake and climbed up on the Bradley.

Before I got inside the hatch I paused a moment to survey the scene. From that height I could see better than I could at ground level. As far as I could see behind us lay miles upon miles of vehicles of all types. There were HUMVEE's, tanks, TOC's, mortar tracks, and trucks large and small for as far as I could see to the southern horizon. To the east and west was a similar scene except mostly there were M3 Bradleys and M1A1 tanks. The whole of the 7th Corps was there. At once I felt better. In front of us was the 2nd ACR moving toward the cuts in the berm. I began to feel sorry for the Iraqi soldier who was going to see this sight coming at him.

We received the order to move and found our place in line moving toward the berm. The berm of sand that had been pushed up by the Iraqis was about ten feet high. As we approached the berm the column began to slow down. When my Bradley was third in line to go through the berm the line stopped. Great! I thought. What a place to be stopped. The one place I *didn't* want to stop and here we are like sitting ducks waiting for incoming artillery to hit us.

Shortly, but not soon enough for my liking, we were moving again. We crossed through the cut in the berm and proceeded to fan out as planned, keeping in tracks already made by the 2nd ACR. The crossing now seemed anticlimactic. I could see trucks and HUMVEE's from the 2nd ACR moving north in front of us. The light blue sky was crystal clear. There was little wind and the temperature was cool. Even with the chemical suit on I didn't feel hot. Out of the corner of my left eye I saw a Humvee quickly approaching my Bradley. A two-star general began to wave at me to stop. The situation seemed like one out of a comic book.

Why was a two-star general trying to stop my Bradley? I surmised that we might be moving into a minefield or something so we stopped to find out. I climbed out of my hatch and got as close to the side as I could without climbing down. I pulled off my CVC helmet so that I could here what he had to say. The general and an aide got out of the HUMVEE and approached me. The general had a microphone in his hand; his assistant had a video camera. He asked me what it felt like to be in Iraq and if we had any problems getting through the berm.

Just then my driver popped his head out of the drivers' hatch and said SFC Z wanted us to get back in formation. I quickly told the general that I had to go, jumped back in the hatch and told the driver to move out. I looked back over my left shoulder and saw the general and his aide standing in the desert looking perplexed. I called SFC Z and told him what had happened; I was moving and would be back in formation shortly. I couldn't understand why the general wanted to interview me. He should have been talking with the first crew through the berm from the 2nd ACR.

As we moved through the desert, I was disappointed with our slow movement. We were only traveling five mph initially. The platoon was in a linear formation forming a line from west to east. My position in the formation was on the far right. The PSG and PLD were both in the middle. After a few hours the 2nd ACR began to pivot to the right and soon there were no more vehicles in front of us. A radio message from LT Wynn told us that we were to take our weapons off safe. There were no more friendlies in front of us. I swallowed a lump in my throat.

I felt naked. There were no more tracks in the sand to follow. I scanned the Iraqi desert near to far intently with my binoculars. SGT Beets scanned the desert with his turret sights. Suddenly a loud explosion ripped the sky. It sounded like it was close by. I asked SGT Beets to tell me if he saw anything. My mouth watered and my heart raced. SFC Z asked everyone for a SITREP (Situation Report). Then I saw it.

A huge black plume of smoke rose from the ground to our right front over a mile away. Sergeant Z had seen it too. He wanted me to tell him what I saw. I keyed my microphone and began to tell him that we were seeing the same thing, but the words caught in my throat. My mortality was suddenly apparent. Were we driving into an ambush? SGT Beets switched to the night sight to get a different look at the situation. He could see an ammunition truck burning and one of its crew rolling on the sand in flames. I called it in to Sergeant Z. LT Wynn then said that our sister unit to the east had fired a tank at this truck and destroyed it. Ammunition from the truck continued to explode. We were ordered forward.

"Keep your eyes peeled" came the admonition over the radio. No one had to tell me. If an ammunition truck, which is usually *behind* combat vehicles, had just been engaged then there must be combat vehicles nearby.

It was soon after this that we approached our first terrain feature, a small hill that only my Bradley would have to go over. To the left of it the desert was flat where the rest of the platoon would move. I told Sergeant Z that I would need to slow down while I moved over this hill. I wanted to move to the right where I would not be so exposed, but I would then be in front of our sister element on the right. There was the possibility that they could mistake us for the enemy and engage us. The hill was a small one with a rut through the middle where vehicles had passed before. It was dangerous to put men on the ground and our forward progress forbade it. I wished that I were authorized to do a recon-by-fire, where direct fire would be directed in the general area where the enemy was suspected. This would force them to either return fire at a distance or keep their heads down while we approached. We had already been told that we were only authorized to fire at clearly identified enemy targets. I knew at this closed-in area we were about to pass through, foot soldiers could approach our vehicle easily.

If I buttoned up (got inside the vehicle and closed the hatch) our field of vision would be severely limited. My problem was that a Bradley commander does not have any weapons except for his pistol. I asked the crew in the back to hand me the M16/203 with a bandoleer of 40mm HE rounds for the grenade launcher and two magazines of ammo for the M16. My heart pounded in my ears as I loaded both of the weapons and took the safety off. In all of my years of training I knew this was the most dangerous thing a combat vehicle could do. Many times over the years my vehicle had been shot in training in just this same scenario.

As we slowly moved up the trail my gunner scanned to our immediate front as I scanned the immediate area to the sides. As we approached the crest I asked the driver to stop while I scanned the area on the other side. Sergeant Z called to say he could now see the backside of the hill and that it was clear. We were now behind the rest of the platoon and needed to catch up. We accelerated down the backside of the hill and caught up to the other Bradleys. I kept the M16/203 on top of the Bradley with me.

Shortly thereafter I came upon a blacktop road running generally east to west. I called it in. As I scanned the area I noticed the asphalt had been torn up at one point. Looking closer at this area I noticed the distinctive marks of a Soviet built tank tread which had bit into the asphalt and surrounding sand. It looked as if the tank had made a U-turn and headed back north. I called it in. My heart almost stopped. This tank could be watching us right now, ready to pull the trigger.

We stopped for a moment while all the gunners in the platoon scanned with their sights and the Bradley commanders scanned with their binoculars. Any hint of the enemy was scrutinized with every means available. We could see nothing. We moved on.

Shortly thereafter we did a refuel on the move. This is a somewhat dangerous mission, but one that allowed the whole unit to keep moving while all the vehicles got topped off with fuel. The first part of this maneuver is the most dangerous-for the fuel tanker drivers. The fuel tankers are huge lumbering fuel trucks loaded with diesel fuel, similar to those you see on American highways. The main differences were that these trucks could travel cross-country and had a sand camouflaged paint job. Initially the whole unit would slow to a crawl. As this was happening the fuel tankers would push ahead of us, park and get ready to refuel. These soldiers were now between us and the enemy on trucks with thousands of gallons of diesel fuel and a five-pound fire extinguisher for each. These soldiers had my admiration. Later, my admiration would grow.

As we approached the fuel tankers, spread out six wide, one vehicle would pull up and receive as much fuel as they could get in five minutes. After that time the fuel would be cut off and the next vehicle would pull up and get their fuel as the first vehicle moved on. This would continue until all of the vehicles had received fuel.

We did all of this without radio traffic so that if the enemy did have a capability to find our location using radio frequencies they would not be able to pinpoint our location. As we approached the fuel tankers I got the Bradley as close as I could. As soon as the driver stopped I unplugged my CVC helmet and climbed out of the hatch. As prearranged, one of my soldiers in the back opened the back door and grabbed the hose from the fueler. As the fueler attached the antistatic line to the Bradley I opened the fuel cover and unscrewed the lid. My crewman pulled the hose to the Bradley and handed it up to me. As soon as I stuck the fuel nozzle into the fuel tank I pulled on the handle and diesel flooded out of the nozzle, some of it right back at me. Droplets of diesel fuel now permeated my chemical protective suit. I wondered if the diesel would affect the protective quality of the suit. Five minutes went quickly. We reversed the order of our movements and moved out. To my left I could see that most of my platoon had finished at about the same time.

Nightfall was now quickly approaching. A little further on we were told that we would be setting up for the night. We closed in on each other to form a shorter line. The LT then told us to set up an AA (assembly area) near some sand berms to our left. We set up in a very tight circle, with each Bradley pointing out. Each vehicle would have someone on watch for two hours at a time, scanning with the night sight and monitoring the radio. The LT told us the 2nd ACR was in a fight near the border with Kuwait. To the east of us we could see light yellow flashes from the guns and hear the fighting. I was glad it was them and not us. I was confident, as were the rest of the platoon, that they would not allow the Iraqis to break through.

I walked outside the perimeter to a sand berm just as the sun was setting. As soon as I stopped my body quivered and I threw up everything in my stomach. I don't know why. I didn't feel nervous or upset. I didn't feel nauseous. I was just walking over to the berm to urinate. I looked around to see if anyone had seen me. I finished what I had to do, went to my Bradley to clean up and ate my supper.

I put myself on watch from 1AM to 3AM and told Specialist Burns to wake me when his watch was through. I climbed into my sleeping bag and instantly went to sleep. At about 12:45AM SPC Allen awakened me. It was dark and cool with countless stars in the sky. I walked over by the berm and again did my business. As I stepped over sleeping bodies in the back of the Bradley I heard the snoring of some very tired soldiers. Pulling myself up into the turret I suddenly felt alone. The radio was silent. There was no need to make a radio check. With all the Bradleys in close proximity it was unlikely all the radios would go down at once. It only took one soldier to hear a radio transmission and he would inform the rest of us by voice.

The fighting by the 2nd ACR had died away. Scanning through the red glow of the night sight it was clear that there was nothing out there. I had saved some of my mail to read for times just like this. Most of the platoon had read every-thing they had received. I found the large manila envelope my mother had sent and opened it. I pulled out a large piece of paper that had been folded several times. On the ends scotch tape had been folded over and I wondered why. My mother had enclosed a letter and I slowly read pieces of it as I periodically checked the night sight. I opened the hatch to listen from time to time.

Her letter told me what had been happening in my hometown. She had cut out articles from the only newspaper in town that told everyone I was in the Mid-dle East. She had gone to the newspaper and asked if they could make a banner for me. They said they could. After it was made my mother put it on display so that friends and family could sign it. Once that was done, she sent it to me. I opened the large piece of paper, which I now recognized as a banner, and spread it out as far as I could inside the turret. On it were printed the words "Delbert, We Are Proud Of You" in large print. All over the banner were the well wishes and signatures of many from my hometown I had known for decades.

I unfolded the banner again and again until I reached the other end reading the kind words of those I knew and loved. Their kind words and moral support touched me. As I sat in this vast desert 7,000 miles from this little town I won-dered if they knew what I was going through. I wondered what the coming day would bring. I knew at some point we would battle the Republican Guard. I wondered what they would do if I returned in a flag-draped coffin. I shook that thought out of my head and checked my watch. In a few minutes I would wake up the next soldier to do his two hours.

As I sat contemplating life in general I opened the hatch and sat on top of the Bradley. I looked up at the vastness of the desert sky. In the blue-black sky were countless stars and galaxies. I took in a deep breath of the cool night air and held it for a moment. I went over in my head the procedures for applying a bandage to a sucking chest wound, applying a tourniquet, and treating a head wound. I thought about the symptoms of dehydration, also chemical and biological attack. I rehearsed my fire commands and took a look at my watch. It was time to wake Burns. It would be time for the crew to wake in two hours. The first twenty-four hours were over.

11

Bedouins, Camels And The Republican Guard

We got up just as dawn was breaking. After a quick cold breakfast, some of it eaten on the move, we were again headed north. We formed up in a linear formation again, however we spread out with about one thousand meters (about ½ mile) between each vehicle. As we moved along we could clearly make out something in the distance. It was soon determined to be a group of Bedouins in pitched tents surrounded by about sixty sheep. I was perplexed. I hadn't seen a blade of grass or a puddle of water since entering Iraq.

I wondered how all of these sheep could have enough water and food to make this trek across the desert. As we got nearer we had no idea if they meant us any harm. They might be soldiers dressed as nomads waiting to ambush us. SGT Beets scanned the group to see if they carried any weapons or looked suspicious. He saw nothing. The Bedouins just stared as we passed by. I wondered what they must have been thinking. Had they ever seen combat vehicles? I was sure they had never seen anything like the Seventh Corps.

We began to see small, brightly colored, cylindrical objects with tail fins lying on the desert floor. Near them was what looked like a bomb, which had been cut in half, and emptied of its contents. I had never seen them before but I recognized this scene as the aftereffects of a CBU (cluster bomb unit) strike. I called it in so that followon units would be careful not to run over them. I wondered what target they had spotted? I could see nothing that would warrant the dropping of a bomb. The desert was as barren as an empty plate.

As we moved along we began to pivot slightly to the northeast. When this happened the Bradley on the far left had to speed up while the Bradley on the far right, my Bradley, had to slow to a crawl. All the Bradleys between the two out-side Bradleys tried to keep in line with the others. As we moved along I couldn't help being awed by the vastness of this desert. A small group of camels loped along in front of us moving east to west a couple of miles away. It figured that animals would scurry before us. Instead they just totally ignored us. I thought we were the biggest, baddest things the world had ever seen. I was put in my place by a bunch of camels.

We saw in the distance a string of high voltage power lines running generally northwest to southeast. It seemed surreal and out of place that something so big, so high-tech would be in a desert which seemed so backward. These power lines were strung on giant metal towers rising almost 100 feet in the air, just like you would see in the United States, with two outstretched metal arms and four metal legs. We called it in so that the helicopters would be certain of seeing it before they came near. As we moved nearer we scanned the towers to see if snipers or explosives had been positioned there. We didn't see anything of concern. As we moved under the high voltage power lines we could here the hum of the electric-ity moving through the lines. A few birds could be seen landing on the towers. I hadn't seen birds since I had seen the one in Saudi Arabia that landed on my tent rope.

The wind began to pick up. The LT said that blowing sand was expected from now on, blowing from the south to the north. Initially I didn't like the thought of blowing sand. In the desert it gets into everything. It gets in your clothes, your equipment, your food. If you are ever offered food with a salting of desert sand and grit, trust me and pass on the opportunity. But the more I thought about it the better I liked it.

On my map I could see we were getting closer to the Republican Guard posi-tions. We were scheduled to attack them the next day early in the morning. The sand would be blowing in their faces and we would be hard to see. Even with goggles it would be difficult. Without them it would be almost impossible. Within a few minutes eyes become filled with sand, stung over and over again by microscopic sand particles. This constant pounding makes eyes dry out, turn red and swollen. When looking through optical sights the scene is clearer, however there is a brown haze that softens the edges of everything you see. You have to use your imagination to see the real image.

Sometimes your imagination plays tricks with your eyes. You see things that aren't there or mistake a tank for a sand dune. We were now approaching low rolling sand dunes. I saw something to my right front. It was just a speck, but it seemed out of place. I alerted my gunner to look in that direction. SGT Beets said he saw someone walking towards us off to the right. He looked unarmed. I called it in. As we closed the distance between the man and us we could tell he was in a military uniform, but was carrying nothing. He didn't even have a helmet. He just continued to walk south in our general direction, shuffling along, seemingly oblivious to our presence.

As we passed him to the right of us about one hundred yards away I felt pity for him. What he must have been through! The constant bombing, the lack of sleep, the supply convoys destroyed; all these things must have taken their toll. The dismounts in the back wanted me to throw him a bottle of water and an MRE. It seemed like the right thing to do, but we had already passed him. I asked them to hand me a bottle of water and MRE for the next one I saw coming toward us in the distance.

As the next man approached I tossed him the bottle of water and MRE. He seemed surprised so I smiled to him and made an exaggerated motion as if I was eating. He made a puzzled, hopeful face, then stuck the MRE under his arm as he opened the small bottle of water. The LT called the radio net to say that we were to save our water and MREs. The supply trains had ample supplies and would take care of these men. Others would process them as POWs. We were to keep moving.

The wind blew harder. We saw no more POWs. The battalion radio net told us that the helicopters would now be moving forward of us to check out the area to our front. A little while later we were told that it had been decided to attack the Republican Guard now rather than in the morning. Now? My heart almost stopped. It was still daylight.

We hadn't refueled. The wind was blowing so hard that even we had a hard time seeing what was in front of us. Our only advantage would be our gunners' night sight. It had a little trouble detecting differences in heat variations in the daytime since the sun had warmed everything to almost the same temperature. After the sun went down the heat signatures of men and vehicles would be much more apparent. The heat loss from the sand would be faster than that of the vehicles. Men would stand out like human torches. Our advantage in the Bradleys at that moment would be extremely thin.

The helicopters had better sights, similar to those in the tanks. They would need to be our initial eyes. Being above would also allow them to see much more of the enemy positions. The republican guard, we had been told, would dig a pit with a bulldozer to serve as their fighting position. Then they would push up sand in front of their vehicles to a point that would totally obscure the vehicle except for a part of the turret and main gun. It was extremely difficult to spot them from the front. The one thing we might be able to see was the defense they had erected to protect their tanks from side attacks by antitank missiles. These were nothing more than pieces of pipe welded together into a rectangular shape with pieces of chain link stretched over them. These would be stuck in the sand using pipe legs that had been welded on. The theory was that if an antitank missile were headed for the tank it would hit the wire and detonate the warhead before it could hit the tank. However, when these defenses were seen, it was a dead giveaway that there was a tank position nearby.

The helicopters radioed the front line trace of the enemy positions. This gave us the direction the enemy guns were pointing. We adjusted our formation to mirror the right flank of the enemy positions. As we approached we were told to slow to a crawl. The helicopters let us know how close we were getting. We could still see nothing. The attack helicopters could see many target opportunities and asked for permission to engage them. Permission was denied. The element of surprise would be gone. The helicopters were pulled back.

As we slowly approached the Iraqi Republican Guard positions we were frustrated that we could see nothing. We knew they were in front of us. "Contact!" boomed a voice over the radio. This was the signal that someone had seen the enemy. It was the Bradley on the far left, SSG Fariello's Bradley. Something could be seen but it was unclear exactly what it was. We were told to keep moving. "Contact!" came another voice over the radio. This time it was SSG Clendenon's Bradley. He was just to the right of the first Bradley. Again it was unclear what they were seeing, but there were at least two things out there that were not natural. We kept moving forward.

To my front I saw a steel fence post sticking in the ground. Further on I saw another one. I called it in. It was the only thing my crew could see. As I passed close by the first post I suddenly remembered we had used them in the past, but only twice. We had used them to mark the maximum range of our weapons so that we would know instantly if we could hit the enemy. These posts had also been used for TRP's (Target Reference Points), points on the ground that had already been zeroed in by the mortars or artillery. All a soldier needed to do was see us near this post and call in a prearranged fire command. The mortars or artillery could begin firing within seconds of this call.

The PSG and PLD both called "contact" in secession. My wingman now called "contact". We still had nothing. I nervously called to SGT Beets to ask if he could see anything. "Nothing", was the reply. It was now dusk. SFC Z now called me to ask if I could see any targets. I told him no. We moved closer. SSG Fariello radioed that his target was a truck. SSG Clendenon radioed that his target was an armored personnel vehicle. He requested permission to engage. He was denied.

Lt. Wynn wanted me to have a target before we began to engage. We crept forward closer and closer to the enemy positions. SGT Beets said he had a target. I looked at the direction of the gun tube. It was pointed directly in front of my wingman, SGT McCulloch. If SGT McCulloch was to move forward even a few feet there was the possibility that we could hit his Bradley. I told SGT Beets the situation and told him to scan only our right front and gave him range limits that would prevent fratricide. These limits could be found inside on the turret ring. SGT Beets sounded frustrated. So was I. We both wanted a target.

Another sweep of the situation to our front found no other targets. We called it in. The PSG sounded frustrated that we hadn't acquired a target. On the battalion radio net we heard the battalion commander order two tanks forward to the left side of the platoon to check things out with their sights. As these tanks moved forward SSG Clendenon and SSG Fariello continued to call in reports. They could see men moving on the ground. It was apparent that we hadn't been seen or heard. Some were sitting down; others were wandering around like an afternoon walk in a park.

The tanks pulled up near the two Bradleys on the far left side, a little forward of them. They radioed in what they saw. There was no aggressive action toward us. No one asked for permission to fire from the Battalion Commander. We were ordered to stop. SGT Beets raised the TOW missile system. The next few seconds seemed like an eternity. The Battalion Commander finally came on the radio. He wanted to know why no one had asked permission to fire. Someone came on the air and reminded him that the enemy hadn't made a move toward us. What if they really wanted to surrender?

The Battalion Commander sounded frustrated with his soldiers and made a short speech about the reason we were here. We were here to kill the enemy. "Now I want you to kill these sons of bitches," he said. A tank round boomed toward the enemy positions. Every gunner watched to see what the Republican Guard would do. Wham! The tank round hit an (APC) armored personnel carrier. The vehicle exploded in a fireball. The Iraqis were stunned, but then began running for their vehicles and bunkers.

The two tanks and all the Bradleys to my left began to fire. SSG Clendenon's gunner, SGT Keaton, began firing at a truck, but couldn't bring himself to destroy it until all of the soldiers had jumped off. Even then most of his rounds went harmlessly through the cloth tarp covering the back of the truck. Just then his main gun jammed. One of the tank gunners patiently waited while Iraqi soldiers piled into the back of his target, another APC. As soon as the back door was closed he put a round right through the middle of it. He watched it hit the APC, blowing the hatches and doors off as it hit the vehicle. Two soldiers fell out of the back of the APC, one of them on fire.

Flames began to grow inside the APC, and then an explosion rocked it, throwing pieces of it high into the sky. The rest of the battalions' tanks were ordered forward to engage the enemy. As they began to move forward we were told to pull back and guard the company TOC. My crew had rehearsed this move. As the driver put the Bradley in reverse, the gunner kept the gun pointed towards the enemy and lowered the TOW missile system. I told SGT Beets to launch the smoke grenades to cover our move. This is one thing we had never done. It was unknown if they even worked.

The grenades launched forward of our position and began to spew thick white smoke. I remained outside of the hatch where I could see what was happening. The last thing I wanted was for us to run into a tank or my wingman. The PLD radioed that his turret power had gone out. He would have to manually hand crank the turret 180 degrees while the driver reversed and turned around. This was a challenging thing to do. It was physically taxing and mentally exhausting. And it took time.

The PSG radioed that his Bradley would stay with him to provide covering fire until the turret was in position. Without the gun pointing away from the M1A1 tanks approaching us from the rear, the PLD could be mistaken for an enemy APC and engaged. At just that moment my Bradley was turned around and heading for the TOC. I waived the bright orange card the commander had given me at the tanks approaching us. An M1A1 tank approaching me was moving his main gun back and forth scanning the area. The 120mm gun stopped when it pointed at my Bradley. Time stood still.

My world stopped. There was a lump in my throat as big as an apple. One pull of the trigger and we would be history. The tanks' gunner quickly jerked the gun away. Simultaneously an artillery airburst lit up the sky above me. I decided it was time to close my hatch and trust SPC Chamberlain, my driver, to find his way to the TOC. I knew once the hatch was closed my vision through the vision blocks would be very limited. As we bumped along I told SPC Chamberlain that I couldn't see a thing, that we were all depending on him to get us to the TOC. "I'll find it Sergeant Abbott," he said. He seemed to be smiling or even laughing as he said it. I had to smile myself. We seemed to be out of the thick of it. We hadn't even fired a shot.

As we moved toward the TOC we fell in behind another Bradley. The radio crackled that the PLD was pulling out and returning to the TOC. We could hear the tanks firing main gun, fifty caliber and coax weapons. Outgoing artillery and mortar fire flew overhead. It was about this time that the mortar platoons FCO (Fire Control Officer) was killed. The crew of the vehicle he was on said he had a premonition of his own death. Before the battle he had put on the CVC vest, which protected crewmen from spall, then added a flak vest on top of it for added protection. As he stood in the open hatch of a mortar track doing his job, the rest of the crew bent down inside the track to hand rounds back to the gun crew. Just then an artillery airburst rent the air and a bomblet hit and killed him. It was determined that the round which had killed him was probably a "short round", a round from one of our own artillery pieces which had not fired as far as it should have.

As we approached the TOC we were told to form a 180-degree arc toward the enemy and scan the area to protect it. We scanned the area and saw the awesome firepower being unleashed. The units on our left and right now joined the battle. Targets were being engaged two and three times to make sure they were destroyed. The Iraqi infantry would try to attack on foot toward our front line and were mowed down shortly after they left their bunkers.

One tank gunner squeezed the trigger on his coax at some infantry exiting a bunker just as they began to raise their hands. By the time he realized they were surrendering, several of them were dead or wounded. The rest ran back inside the bunker and waited for daylight. Another gunner played with the Iraqi infantry exiting the bunkers. He would lay a burst of coax fire in front of the first man out. As the group would run back the other way he would fire a burst at the other end of the group. He figured they would throw down their weapons and give up. They wouldn't! After firing several bursts at each end, and realizing they would neither retreat or surrender, he cut them down where they stood.

The tanks were now running out of fuel. Our Bradleys were still OK, but M1A1 tanks get 8 gallons per mile on the average. No, not 8 miles per gallon; 8 gallons per mile! The engine needed to be turning to keep the batteries charged. With the turret being continually operated the batteries would discharge quickly. We would soon have tanks that couldn't move or shoot. The commander ordered the fuel tankers forward. As I looked in disbelief the fuel tankers moved to the rear of the tanks and refueled them as the tanks continued to fire and artillery lit the sky.

These fuel handler soldiers were braver than anyone I had ever seen. We were under armor, with guns and missiles to protect us. They were totally exposed, pouring fuel from a large fuel tank, in the middle of a firefight. These guys had my highest respect. As the fight went on I could see we were in no danger of being overrun. Airbursts of our artillery twinkled as it burst over the enemy in the night sky. All tank firing had stopped. The radio was silent. I suddenly felt very tired and hungry. I saw that the rest of the crew had finished eating. I told my gunner to take over. I was going to get something to eat and get some rest. I told him to wake me if he needed me. I crawled down from the turret and ate a cracker and drank some water. I crawled into a corner, pulled a blanket over me and fell into a deep sleep.

12

Clearing Bunkers And Destroying Tanks

I awoke to a new day. SGT Beets had moved the track while I slept because the platoon had adjusted position during the night. As I washed my hands and ate breakfast I took a look around. We hadn't moved far. But everything looked different in the daylight. As the sun came up Iraqi soldiers began surrendering. I could see a simple two-strand enclosure behind us about a thousand yards that held many prisoners. Others were walking by us to the west toward this enclosure accompanied by no one, their hands held high or behind their heads. SFC Z walked over to me and said that the Lt.'s Bradley was still down. He would need to use my Bradley today since the platoon was tasked on a mission. My crew would stay with his Bradley and help the mechanics fix it.

I suggested that perhaps the LT could use my wingman's' Bradley so that I could go on the mission. He immediately said it had already been decided and to get my crew over to the Lt.'s Bradley. Disappointed, I told my crew to move their gear over to the other Bradley. They were just as disappointed. I felt as if I had let my crew down, that somehow I wasn't worthy of the day's mission.

Then I remembered that this is the way it was supposed to be. My wingman's Bradley didn't have a second radio so that the LT could monitor the Battalion radio net. In the line of secession the LT would always get my Bradley if his went down. I felt a little better but still felt alienated from the rest of the platoon. My crew took the LT's Bradley back to the bone yard and parked it. That is when I saw we weren't the only ones. SSG Clendenin's Bradley was there as well as several other vehicles. For the remainder of the day we washed ourselves, changed clothes, and cleaned our weapons.

The next morning Lt. Wynn's' Bradley had been repaired, as well as SGG Clendenon's and we prepared to move out. We had been told to move to the far side of the defensive position where the Republican Guard had been attacked. A way had been cleared through the minefield and graves registration had removed the bodies of the Iraqis the day before. We were to move to positions facing east, just north of the Kuwait border. Our mission was to watch for any Iraqi units moving north out of Kuwait and engage them if they moved toward us.

We moved single file through the minefield, the Lt in the lead. While we moved, Lt. Wynn talked to us on the radio. When we had cleared the minefield he noted that he must be the luckiest Lieutenant in the Army. We had maneuvered across a vast empty desert, found the enemy and made it this far without any casualties. We all breathed a sigh of relief. As we moved in front of the Republican Guard positions, I got an uneasy feeling as we passed their tanks, most undamaged, with their gun tubes pointed at us. I knew that we had rounded up many prisoners the previous day, but just suppose there was one with a death wish. Could anybody be certain that every tank was empty?

I breathed a sigh of relief as we moved past their positions. We took up our new positions facing east. The Bradleys were placed about 50 yards apart with our dugouts between them. Once everything was set, we were told to prepare for a mission to clear the Iraqi bunkers and destroy any Iraqi vehicles, especially tanks, that had not been destroyed during the battle. This was a mission for the dismounts, SPC's Allen and Burns. They were giddy that they were finally getting to do something besides ride in the back of the Bradley. I was going along to supervise the mission for my men. We were given thermite grenades to place on the rear deck of the Iraqi tanks, which would burn through the engine block when ignited. I grabbed my Iraqi phrase book and memorized a couple of phrases to coach the Iraqis out of their bunkers if needed. I didn't want to kill an Iraqi just because he was frightened.

It was a fun mission, one that Burns and Allen said upon our return to Germany that they enjoyed the most. The Iraqis living conditions were similar to those we now occupied. In each hole was found a thin mattress, empty food tins and assorted trash. We found no Iraqis hiding there. I was surprised that I didn't see any bomb craters or destroyed tanks behind the front lines. We had the impression that this unit had been hit over and over again by the Air Force from the many reports we had heard on the radio, but we saw no evidence of it.

I felt almost giddy as I climbed aboard the first tank to disable it. I had my sunglasses on as I pulled the pin on the thermite grenade. I should have jumped off the tank at that point, but I wanted to see the grenade burn through the metal of the tank. Just then, a small spark from the grenade hit the left lens of my sunglasses and burnt a small hole in it. I quickly jumped down and was thankful I had chosen to wear my glasses that day. We all returned to the platoon satisfied in the knowledge that we had helped destroy Iraqi tanks and there were no more Iraqi soldiers to make trouble for us.

13

The Last Watch

That night I had taken the last night watch. No one had seen anything during their watch. I doubted I would either. I scanned my limits with the night sight; nothing. Everyone was sleeping soundly for the first time in days, except those of us on watch. I decided to get a jump on breakfast and opened an MRE. Every few minutes I would look through the night sight and scan the area. It seemed pointless.

My mind began drifting, remembering the previous days, estimating how long it would take to get home. I looked through the night sight again; nothing. I wondered how things were back in the States. I wondered when we would get mail again. I took out one more letter to read. I had one more saved. I would save it for the day after tomorrow. After reading the letter I felt a little better. There were kind words and best wishes. But it was clear the writer didn't have a clue what we were going through and seemed like it had been written in another decade.

I scanned the area to my front to the horizon again. At almost the end of my scan, near the horizon, I saw a small red dot. I scanned past it and back to the red dot. Huh, I said to myself. I knew that hadn't been there on my last scan. I focused the night sight to get a better picture. No matter how I focused, it was still a small red dot. I switched to the day sight. Darkness flooded the sight. The sun would not be coming up for several minutes. I switched back to the night sight. The dot didn't look like it had moved. I noted the azimuth and elevation reading on my turret settings. Whatever it was, it was a long way off. I finished my breakfast and made another scan.

Now there were two dots in the same location. The first dot had moved slightly to the left. The second dot was now in its place. Whatever it was, it was moving north at a great distance from us. I was torn between letting someone know what I was seeing and letting everyone sleep. I knew the first thing the chain of command would want to know was what was I seeing? At this point I couldn't tell. Until they got closer or the sun came up, so that I could use the daysight, I wouldn't know.

Any report sent forward would probably be sent up the chain and scrutinized. Calls would then be sent down to me every few minutes to find out what I was seeing. The whole division could be put on alert. I remembered when I was stationed in Germany during the Cold War. NATO had been put on alert because of a similar situation. Thousands of troops manning tanks, APC's, trucks, HUM-VEE's, planes and helicopters had been shaken out of bed and deployed to their battle positions. A scout had seen something in a field on the other side of the border that hadn't been there previously. Constant calls were made to him by higher command. What is it? The scout didn't know. Later, what is it? He repeated that he didn't know. He wouldn't know until the sun came up.

Again, they wanted to know what it was. He kept repeating that he didn't know. Frustrated, the commander asked him to make an educated guess as to what it was he was seeing. The scout didn't want to guess. That wasn't his job. He was to report what he heard and saw. Guesses were to be done by the officers. The commander forced the issue. The scout finally relented and told him he thought it could possibly be a couple of tanks. The company commander put his troops on alert and sent the information up the chain of command. The next higher command saw the information and put his soldiers on alert also. It kept going like that until all of NATO was put on alert.

As the sun came up over the horizon the scout finally could see what the lumps were that he had seen. In the dawn light he could clearly see two large stacks of hay that the local farmer had put there on top of a hill just as the sun had been going down. Those of us who had been put on alert were not amused. The alert had cost the military hundreds of thousands of dollars and shaken the confidence of thousands of soldiers in their leadership.

I doubted that the same thing would happen to me. But even the possibility that it could happen again and the realization that we were in no present danger, made me keep the information to myself. I scanned again. I could now see five red dots just below the horizon. I adjusted my nightsight over and over again to try and get a better picture. They were still just five red dots moving north very slowly.

The sun was beginning to come up. The sky began to turn from blue-black to a dark blue-gray. I switched to my daysight. Below the horizon everything was still black. I switched back to the nightsight. The dots were growing slightly bigger now and there were more of them. I began to get concerned. Since the dots were getting bigger I knew that they were now moving a little closer to us. However the dots to the left were bigger than the ones on the right. This indicated that they were not moving directly at us but at an angle, approximately north-northwest. From our latest briefing I knew there were none of our troops to our north that would be in danger. At this point our unit was deployed the farthest east of any friendly unit in Iraq.

I scanned the dots again. They were slightly larger now. Our soldiers were now being awakened. As my crew unzipped their sleeping bags and rubbed their eyes I checked the nightsight again. As I focused the nightsight I could now see a faint outline. I flipped to my daysight. I could now see that dust was being kicked up behind the blurry objects. There were now about twenty-five objects. I felt a little relief. With the platoon waking up, I knew that if what I was seeing was an Iraqi unit and it turned to engage us, we had plenty of time to man our guns and TOW missiles before they were in range. I watched my crew as they ate their breakfast then returned to my scanning.

The nightsight could now see more distinct images. It certainly didn't look like any vehicles I had ever seen. I flipped to the daysight, which had a more powerful sight. As I adjusted the focus I could now see that there were about thirty shapes moving across the desert moving north-northwest. The dust cloud had now grown bigger. It obscured the outlines of the objects. I knew that in the next few minutes I would need to identify these objects and call it in. My heart pounded in my ears.

One of my crew asked me a question and I turned to answer him, trying to act nonchalant. My whole being begged to have my eye plastered on the eyepiece trying to identify what was there. I wrapped up my conversation with the man and quickly pushed my eye up against the eyepiece. The shapes were almost visible now. I focused the nightsight again. The odd shapes confused me. What in the world was I seeing? I had seen all kinds of vehicles through these sights. Nothing registered as being familiar. I switched to the daysight. The sky on the horizon had now turned to a light blue-gray with a brown haze engulfing the shapes. I found one shape at the front of the group that was slightly bigger than the rest without the brown haze obscuring its outlines. As I focused the eyepiece a distinctive shape emerged.

I began to chuckle to myself. I wiped my eye with my hand, wiped the condensation from the eyepiece with a piece of lens paper and took another look. I confirmed what I had just seen. My whole countenance now relaxed. A big smile grew across my face. I took another look. I could now see several of the other shapes distinctly. They were all the same.

I climbed down out of the turret. It was time for the next man to take his turn. I told him the condensed version of what I had seen and gave him the elevation and azimuth to the shapes in the distance. I was now glad that I hadn't alerted anyone to the sight. I would now be getting ribbed for getting everyone up early for nothing. I went over to SFC Z's hooch and let him know what I had seen. He seemed unconcerned, and rightly so. I wondered if he knew how much I had sweated the whole experience. As I walked back to my Bradley my step was a little lighter. Somehow the air seemed cleaner, the day a little brighter. I shook my head and laughed at myself. I couldn't believe I had gotten so concerned over a herd of camels.

14

The Water Shortage

I don't remember exactly when we got the news that the war was over. All I know is that someone ran from position to position to let us know. Someone had heard it on his radio. It sounded like good news, but I knew better than to get overly excited. We still had a while to go before we would be going home. Even if they began moving units home today, we would not be among them. They would probably send the troops who had been over the longest first. That would be the Eighty Second Airborne. We were one of the last units to be deployed. Later that evening the LT came back from a meeting and said that indeed the coalition forces had decided to stop fighting.

It was then that I realized that we were short of water. SPC burns had wanted to start personal hygiene and I noticed that the water can was almost empty. I checked the others to see how much water we had left. We had about three inches of water in two of our five-gallon water cans and what we had left in our canteens. That was it. I told him to stop. The rest of the water would only be used for drinking.

I walked over and let SFC Z know our situation. The whole platoon was in the same situation. He had already checked on the water supply with headquarters. The water buffalos that were to supply us water were empty and on their way back to the water supply points in Saudi Arabia. We were promised an airdrop of water to take care of us until they arrived. I had confidence in our leadership, but I wondered how long it would take to coordinate such a drop and make it happen. If getting our mail in a timely manner was any indication, I didn't feel good about the results.

I suspected that the large numbers of Iraqi prisoners had overwhelmed the supply system. If supplying these prisoners had not been anticipated and a plan implemented to deal with the situation the Seventh Corps would be in a world of hurt. In the United States the presence of clean drinking water is everywhere. There are water fountains, bottled water, and every other kind of drink imaginable available every few blocks. But here in this vast desert it was nonexistent, except for what was carried. My mouth felt hot and dry. My whole body ached to have a shower. Visions of waterfalls, lakes and streams flashed before my eyes. What a laugh it would be for our enemies to find our dehydrated bodies littering the desert after such a victory!

A couple of hours later I saw dust rising in the south and squinted to make it out. It was a C-130 cargo plane flying just above the desert with a drop chute opening behind it. As it flew by it dropped several palettes of water bottles on the desert floor about a mile behind our position, stirring clouds of dust into the air as it flew. All of us stood up and watched as it happened. A cheer rose from all over the division. Clapping hands punctuated the moment. Now the water was in the hands of the division supply system. The amount of water dropped didn't seem like it would go very far with so many soldiers in the division. I wondered if there had been enough dropped to make a real difference.

A couple hours later a truck came by and gave each Bradley crew a couple boxes of bottled water. Some of the bottles had broken on impact of the cargo drop, so we were told to still ration the water until further notice. We each grabbed a bottle, stuffed it into an army green sock, and dribbled water over the sock to help cool the water in the bottle. We were all thankful that someone had the foresight to send us water in a timely manner. Even though cleaning our bodies would have to wait, we had what we needed to survive and that was all that mattered.

15

Clearing an Iraqi Village

Our platoon was later given the task of clearing a village that was behind our position. We had not received fire from this village, but it is a good idea not to leave a village within a short distance from your position without knowing if there are any "bad guys" there. We mounted our Bradleys and made our way down the dusty road. Clearing a village is a mission usually left to infantry soldiers, not cavalry soldiers. However, it was a small village, was assumed to be friendly, and it seemed like our basic soldier skills could accomplish the mission. In basic training we were taught to cover each other while the other moved, keep a small silhouette, and move fast. We knew that all houses and rooms had to be thoroughly searched for soldiers, weapons and ammunition.

As we approached I saw something that concerned me. A ten-foot wall surrounded the village. No village I had seen had such a wall. If a village did have a wall it was usually not over three feet tall. This village seemed more like a compound or fort than a village. The likelihood that there were bad guys there just increased. Next, it was apparent that the Bradleys would not be able to overwatch our search of the village. Normally if we had to do anything on the ground where we could come in contact with the enemy the Bradleys were positioned where they could fire on the enemy in case we needed more firepower. The only place we could put the Bradleys were at the entrance to the compound.

Trying to take a Bradley through that narrow gate before the compound was cleared could be suicide. The Bradley crew could not see but a narrow section of the compound and was limited to movement on the narrow streets. Clearly it was too risky to take the Bradleys into the compound. We positioned them at the front gate to control movement out of the compound and provide critical overwatch if we had to leave the compound through the gate in a hurry.

The next problem we saw was that the first soldier through that gate would be an instant target. Anyone inside the compound would only have to aim at the gate and pull the trigger when the first soldier came through it. Without knowing the layout of the compound in order to get behind some cover quickly the first soldiers through the gate would be sitting ducks. The NCOIC (Noncommissioned Officer In Charge), SFC Montgomery, decided to use the Bradleys height to its best advantage. He ordered one of the Bradleys to pull next to the wall and put a soldier on top to look over the wall. From this soldier we learned that the compound looked clear. There were trees everywhere, a main street running down the middle of the compound, and a grassy area in the middle void of trees and houses. The houses were all one-story with flat roofs. This soldier could provide some overwatch while we cleared the compound. If anyone got on top of the houses he would know it.

The compound was about four blocks wide by eight blocks long. The OIC (Officer in Charge), Lt. Lloyd, decided that we would take the compound by searching and securing the right side first then taking the other side, the dividing line being the main road. Our adrenaline was pumping as we checked our weapons and gear. The signal was given and the first two men went through the main gate taking up positions on either side of the gate inside the compound. Finding it quiet, the rest of us went through the gate and began to search the houses.

The quiet of the compound was relaxing. The shade of the trees was a welcomed friend in this desert landscape. This would be a cakewalk, I thought. The houses all seemed abandoned with the front doors wide open, papers littering the floors. Something seemed familiar about these houses, but I couldn't quite put my finger on it. Then it hit me. The telephones were just like the ones I had seen in Germany. In some houses there was furniture left behind. It was German, too. I couldn't believe it. I looked at the electrical outlets: German. As I walked out of the next house I saw a car: German. A German car? I thought this place was deserted! Who would leave a nice BMW behind?

Suddenly it felt like eyes were watching us. I thumbed my safety to make sure I could flick it to the fire position, if needed, in a hurry. I pointed out the car to those around me. Then someone else spotted another one. I saw Lt. Lloyd near me, close to the main road in the compound. Our men were almost through clearing the right side and I wanted him to know about the cars we had spotted.

Just as I approached him and began to talk a figure suddenly appeared in a doorway opposite us, in the half of the compound that hadn't been cleared.

My adrenaline shot from zero to off the charts in a split second. Lt. Lloyd and I both swung our weapons in the direction of the doorway, flicking the safety off as we drew down on the man in the doorway. We both realized before we pulled the trigger that this was a noncombatant. It was an old German man walking to the doorway to smoke a cigarette. We both lowered our weapons. My body shuddered slightly as we both let out nervous laughter. Prickly sweat appeared on my forehead then all over my body. The old German man nervously dropped his cigarette, backed excitedly through the doorway and closed the door. We let the rest of the group know that there were civilians in the area. We put our safeties back on as we resumed the search of the area.

The search turned up a few more civilians and a couple more cars, but nothing else. This was one of those missions most combat soldiers live for. There is something about the thrill of having the power of life and death at your fingertips. There is the challenge of finding someone who may be trying to kill you. There is the excitement of seeing new territory and feeling that, at least for the moment, you have complete control of other peoples' lives. It is the John Wayne feeling. Nothing in life is as intoxicating. Yet, in the second that you draw down on a man your humanity comes screeching in to save the day. You realize that you are not ten feet tall. You are only a man with a weapon governed by the rules of humanity and the rules of war.

16

Into The Neutral Zone

My crew was assigned a mission to escort a team of medics into the neutral zone between the Iraqi army and the coalition. We were to be there just as a precaution. We were to accompany the medics as a ready reaction force in case something happened unexpectedly. We were to meet the medic track at a prearranged point and follow them on their mission. The medic track was hard to miss. It was a converted M113 armored personnel carrier with a large white square painted on each side covered by a large red cross.

The medics took the lead as we headed into the neutral zone. As we moved toward a small village in the distance, we came across a small-whitewashed building with one small window near the roof. The building was about the size of an average American living room with an extended thatched roof attached on the far side. It was located next to a ditch that ran along the side of the road. As we approached, the medic track slowed to a stop.

A female voice came on the radio and informed me that there was no need to dismount any men. We were to be ready to dismount, if needed, but armed soldiers would only make the people nervous. I was curious. I had heard of no women in our Battalion. As the medics dismounted I noticed that the lieutenant was a nice looking woman with sandy blonde hair. I checked the bumper markings on the medic track and realized that this crew had been attached from another unit.

As I waited on the medics to do their work I looked around the area. There were simple white curtains on the window. There were sheep around the house. Presently, a young girl of about three or four shyly stepped around the corner of the house. Her hair was filthy, as well as her dress. She was barefoot. Her hair was a tangled mess on her head. But she had wonderful, innocent eyes and a warm smile. A boy with a shaved head, a couple inches taller than the girl ambled around the corner to check out the parade. He was barefoot, too, wearing dirty shorts and a filthy face. But again the beautiful innocent eyes took my focus off the rest. He smiled shyly as he approached the medic track, looking up in my direction. As he walked I noticed feces littering the ground near his feet, some with toilet paper attached.

I reeled in horror as I tried to grasp the situation. When the female medic reappeared, I couldn't read her face, so I asked her if everything was all right. She said the children were sick. There were ten people living in the house as well as the stock animals. Flies were worse inside than they were outside the home. I was shocked to see people living like this. Many domestic animals in the U.S. live in better conditions than this family.

In short order we were moving again. As we moved toward a small village in the distance Sgt Beets scanned the area with the daysight to check for anything of concern. The village looked clear. The medics stopped on the edge of the city and again asked us to stay in the vehicle. I had Sgt Beets scan the next nearest village to see if there was anyone not liking the fact that we were there. As he did some children began walking down a path towards the village where we were to check out what was happening. It was a beautiful day and the children were smiling, laughing, and skipping on the sun drenched pathway. It was wonderful so see the innocence and wonder of children again.

Suddenly, one of the boys walking down the path stopped in place, looked at us and began running in the other direction. The rest of the children joined him. We were puzzled. Why were they running? As I lowered my binoculars, I could clearly see the reason. Since our sights were slaved to the main gun it was also pointing at the little children. Sgt Beets and I were horrified to think that these children thought we were going to shoot them. We quickly moved the turret away from the village and waived our arms to let them know we meant them no harm. It was too late. The damage had been done. It was clear we wouldn't be allowed to visit that village.

After several minutes the woman medic returned to the medic vehicle shaking her head. I could read her face this time. It was a look of being perplexed and horrified. I asked her what she had seen. She said the good thing was that we had come at a good time of day. Any other time when the men were in the village we would not have been welcomed. However, the women of the village welcomed us with open arms since the men were at work in the fields.

The bad thing was what she saw after she was allowed inside. The medic asked if I had seen a young woman in a royal blue dress. I told her I had. She was hard to miss among all of the other women in black and brown burkas. This woman's' husband had caught her looking at another man. No, she wasn't kissing him. She wasn't having sex with him. She was just looking at another man. Her husband had his two other wives take her into the kitchen and hold her down while he cut off one of her breasts.

The medic returned to the village with more medicine. I sat stunned as I thought of what she had just said. After I got my composure I told my men what she had said. We were all stunned. None of us could even imagine someone being so cruel, especially the woman's husband. Shortly the medic returned, almost in tears. She had just seen a young boy with a distended stomach. He was full of worms. He was in such an advanced stage that there was nothing she could do. The little boy would die within days. Caught early, an inexpensive medicine could have saved his life.

This short time with the medics emphasized to me again how we in the United States take so many things for granted. Sanitary living conditions, clean water, and respect for human life are so common in the United States that to see a people without them brings pause.

17

Malaria Pills?

The rumors were flying. Units were redeploying to the states. Some were scheduled to march down streets in tickertape parades. Planeloads were leaving every day. In no time it would be our turn. I tried to keep my soldiers grounded in reality, but nothing worked. I ran the numbers in my head. How long would it take to fly almost one half million men and women from all over the Middle East to their origin? I didn't know exactly, but it had taken months for us to get there. Reversing the procedure would take almost as long, even if there were ways to shorten some of the process. And the fact that we would be returning in the same order we arrived meant that we would be the last unit to return.

The more I tried to reason with my soldiers the less headway I made. Almost everyone in the platoon was walking on air. We're going home! The grins from ear to ear made me feel sick. I wanted to be happy for them, but I knew their balloon would burst. I wanted to be happy, too. I wanted to get out of the desert and see trees again, see civilian women again, have a decent meal and walk around in civilian clothes. I wanted to see my parents and friends. I wanted to drive a car, and have a choice of food and drink. I wanted to watch TV, call someone on the telephone and have a daily shower. There was so much we all wanted. We just wanted to feel normal again.

My confidence was shaken for a minute when we were told to prepare for movement. Were we really going back to Germany? I walked over to the platoon leadership tent and pried for information. Sergeant Z said he didn't know where we were going, but he gave me some pills that each of us were to take prior to moving. "What are the pills for" I asked? "They are malaria pills" was the answer. Malaria pills? "Why would we need malaria pills" I queried? He didn't know but we would find out at the evening meeting when the lieutenant got back from his briefing.

As I walked back to my Bradley I pondered what the malaria pills meant. I couldn't figure it out. The only thing I knew for sure was that there was no reason they would give us these pills if we were going back to Germany. This was the first time in my career I had been ordered to take malaria pills. These pills were commonly issued to soldiers who would be stationed near water where mosquitoes were prevalent. As I watched my men take their pills they made weak arguments that the pills meant we were going home soon. Even after I told them what I knew they wouldn't believe me that we weren't going back to Germany. I felt frustrated. But what could I do?

I waited for the evening briefing and wondered what they would do when I broke the news to them. Their morale would be shot. So would mine. But there are times in life when there is only so much you can do and circumstances take care of the rest. I would have to play it by ear and try to make the most of the situation.

The lieutenant returned well before sunset. Word was sent for Bradley commanders to meet in the command tent. I grabbed my LBE, put on my helmet, grabbed my map and walked over to the tent.

As I walked down into the hand-dug belly of the tent I could see that someone had already rolled the Lt.'s and Sergeant Z's sleeping bags to one end of their cots so that we could sit down. I took a seat on the far end of the Lieutenant's cot as the rest of the vehicle commanders came inside. We all looked at each other with quiet expectation. The Lieutenant continued to stir his coffee. The tension was just too much for SGG Fariello.

"Well Lieutenant, are we going home", he asked? "Not hardly", came the reply, "we are moving north to a point near the Euphrates's river. That is why we were issued the malaria pills." "Why would we be moving north? The war is over Lieutenant", SGT McCulloch said. "We have to relieve a unit that got here well before we did so that they can go home. We have to secure the area so that EOD (Explosive Ordinance Disposal) can collect and destroy ammunition", the Lieutenant explained. We all groaned and felt a pang of disgust. We all knew that this was a mission best left to infantry, if this could be considered a real mission at all.

The Iraqi army was beaten. Any units that remained would not want to fight us. It seemed like busy work. He gave us details on the movement and dismissed us. I slowly walked back to my Bradley. I knew what I would see: smiling faces who would want to know when we were leaving. I decided to tell them when we were leaving then let the enthusiasm die down before I told them where we were moving. Sure enough the smiling faces were there. "We leave in two days", I said. "Alright", Sgt Beets said, high fiving SPC Chamberlain as he did. They all smiled. I let them revel in the moment for a minute without saying a word.

"Is that it", SPC Chamberlain asked? "Not quite", I said, "Do you remember the malaria pills we took"? "Yeah", they all said hesitantly. "We need them because we are going to be near the Euphrates River", I said, letting the idea sink in. "What", several of them said in amazement? The distorted faces and looks of shock told me I had better go slowly with the information. "The Euphrates, where is that", SPC Burns said? "It's north of here", I said. "Well what in the world are we going to be doing up there", SPC Allen said? "We are going to be securing the area so that the EOD team can blow up some ammunition", I said slowly. "Just tell us everything", Sergeant Beets said. He could tell I was serious and knew that we would be there for a while.

I laid my map on the ramp and went through everything I had been told. I suppressed the urge to say, "I told you so". I knew that was the last thing they needed to here. I wanted them to take me seriously when I told them something and they did. But when it came to going back to Germany, many soldiers immediately embraced any rumor about our return, no matter how ridiculous.

Two days later the Lieutenant took the lead since he had the GPS and we headed west. We passed back through our battlefield following a trail that had been cleared through the minefields. As I looked at all of the destroyed tanks, APCs, trucks and antiaircraft guns I realized we had fought a larger unit than I had originally thought. We had hit them from the southwest instead of the southeast, as they were oriented. We had blindsided them, pinned them, and then killed the rest whenever they tried to move.

I was so grateful that our leadership knew how to fight. Throughout history soldiers had been slaughtered by the thousands because their leadership didn't think like fighters. At one point we headed northwest crossing more and more endless desert. Occasionally I would see the outside shell of a CBU (cluster bomb unit) near an antiaircraft site. Some of these had bomblets scattered on the ground that hadn't exploded. I radioed their location and reminded my crew that even though they looked harmless not to go near them. Later we came upon a huge littering of destroyed vehicles and moved around to the other side of them.

Engineers had already dug a place for our platoon nearby. Small bulldozers had created six fighting positions in a semicircle facing north. These fighting positions were called hull downs because the hull of the vehicle was completely hidden, leaving only the turret exposed. This makes the vehicle a small target and gives the crew added protection while it fights. The engineers dug bunkers for us between the vehicles for sleeping and protection with Iraqi backhoes they had found. Our location this time was near a small destroyed building. There wasn't anything of much use to us for building our bunkers, but we used whatever we could find. We continued to have someone on watch to monitor the radios and scan the area to our front. Whenever the EOD or other soldiers were in the area one or two Bradleys would escort them around the area. Occasionally, we would get a warning on the radio that EOD was preparing to explode something and we would get inside the Bradleys and close the hatches until the "all clear" was given.

18

Easter In Paradise

One day Sergeant Z told us he had good news that he would give us at a briefing. Immediately soldiers began to assume that this meant we were going home. I groaned knowing that it was still too soon to get our hopes high. I gave up trying to persuade them that their expectations were unreasonable. Logic has no place in the heart of a young soldier wanting to go home. At the meeting Sergeant Z told us he had secured the Chaplain for an Easter sunrise service. Many of the units in our Battalion had wanted him for the same purpose. Since Sergeant Z had always been close to the Chaplain and the Chaplain had a special place in his heart for front line soldiers he had selected us. No group of soldiers had been on the front line longer than we cavalry scouts.

Sergeant Z wanted to know how we could make this service special. We had no chapel, no chairs, not even a pulpit. He told us to gather everything we could find that might even remotely be used and meet him over at a flat spot just east of our positions. We gathered used water bottles, bricks, an old door and boards. We stacked the bricks from the destroyed building into two legs and laid the old door on top, removing the doorknob. Then he asked to barrow someone's army green blanket and laid it over the door, letting the front side hang down and cover the bricks.

Sergeant Z appeared with two emergency candles and said he needed candle-holders. Sgt Hall suggested that we cut the water bottles in half and fill them with sand, then place the candles in the sand. Sergeant Z agreed. Then we stacked more bricks in front of the altar to form legs for benches. Then we placed the boards on top of these. Granted, it wasn't much but it was better than nothing. We had made do with what we had. It would have to be enough. We hoped the Chaplain would like it.

Early on Easter morning we were wakened by the soldier on watch to see if we wanted to go to the sunrise service. I felt a little groggy and wondered if it would be worth it. I decided almost immediately that no matter how it turned out it was worth getting out of bed early. As I got dressed I pictured our feeble attempt at a worship area and unreasonably compared it to the great cathedrals I had seen in Germany. I knew there was no comparison and that true worship was from the heart. But I couldn't shake the feeling that this service would be less than memorable.

As we waited for the Chaplain to arrive I drank a little water and rubbed the sleep out of my eyes. Soon we could see the headlights of the Chaplains humvee approaching in the distance. The humvee drove into the assembly area after being challenged by a dismount we had posted at the entrance. It wasn't really a challenge. The guard said something that drew chuckles from inside the humvee and the guard waived the Chaplain and his driver through. The humvee stopped near Sergeant Z's bunker and its occupants slowly disembarked. Faces brightened as the Chaplain greeted soldiers waiting for the service. Sergeant Z noted that we had a good turnout but that some couldn't be convinced. "Let them sleep", said the Chaplain, "its OK". The Chaplains driver was directed over to the makeshift altar and began arranging a communion set and other items on it. "Well", said the Chaplain, looking at his watch, "I believe we had better get started".

We all walked over to the altar we had erected, with flashlights pointing the way. As I sat down the concrete and bricks of the bench legs shifted slightly and I wondered if it would remain intact. As we sat uncomfortably on the benches the Chaplain remarked that we had made a fine open air chapel. He hadn't expected it. He was just going to serve communion from the hood of the humvee. He said he appreciated the thoughtfulness of the little chapel and hoped his words would be enough to honor our efforts.

He remarked that out of all the units in the Battalion he wanted to spend Easter sunrise with us. He knew we had risked more, seen more and been through more than any other soldiers in the four hundred strong Battalion. We thirty men held a special place in his heart. The candles were lit and the service began. As the Chaplain repeated words I had heard thousands of times about the resurrection my mind suddenly realized that I was spending Easter in the Middle East, close to where the events actually happened. I remembered that Iraq had once been Babylon where the Israelites had been captives under Nebuchadnezzar. This was the land where the Prophet Daniel had written some of the Bible and where Jonah had warned the people of Nineveh of God's judgment.

The area where the Tigris and the Euphrates meet was where some think the Garden of Eden once stood. There was so much history in this land where we had just fought that it was overwhelming. Gradually the sun began to rise behind the Chaplain. The sky turned from a dark gray to a light yellow, casting the Chaplain into a shadow while everything else brightened. We had survived the war to see another Easter, even though it was not with our family and friends. However, we soldiers felt like a family and many of us were friends. It would have to do until later, much later. As the service closed communion was given.

As I took a small glass of grape juice I reached to hand the platter to a soldier on my right. As I did there was a nudge on my shoulder. I turned around to see one of the soldiers who wanted to sleep gesturing for a glass. As I held the platter so that he could take one I noticed that almost every one of the soldiers who had wanted to sleep was now fully dressed, standing behind me a short distance. I no longer thought about the frailty of our little chapel. Others could have the huge cathedrals, the empty gestures, and the hollow words. We now had something few people ever share.

There was now a sense of history, a sense of destiny, a sense of unity in spirit that is rare in everyday life. We had made it through separation from our families, the scud attacks, and the end run across the Iraqi desert to destroy the Republican Guard. Many more things lay before us before we returned to Germany. But the days ahead seemed much brighter than the ones we had just left.

19

We Watched As Basra Died

After a few days we were given orders to move even farther north. The faces of the men were a lot less excited now when rumors of our departure reached them. We couldn't believe our luck that we were moving further away from where we all wanted to go. As we moved north we began to see short blades of grass scattered in the sand. Occasionally, we would see an Iraqi farm in the distance. These farms were made by bulldozing an area of desert and pushing the sand to about three feet high on every side. Then, fertilizer and topsoil were added. A nearby water well would supply water to flood the farm when needed. These farms were usually three to five acres and looked out of place in the mostly desert terrain.

As we approached the area we were to occupy the soldiers from the unit we were replacing were all smiles. If we couldn't go home yet, at least other units were leaving. We were to take over their positions straddling the main highway, highway eight, from Basra to Baghdad and another road that ran parallel to it. Our mission was to stop any military hardware and troops from going either direction.

My section was positioned on the road running roughly parallel to highway eight. We were to search every vehicle and every person, except women, unless there was an obvious reason to do so. One of the tank platoons would provide security for us while we searched. Their guns were oriented east, toward Basra. A tent was brought to us for sleeping. They didn't want us to dig any more holes. It was getting warmer now during the day. At least now we didn't have to wear the chemical suits.

As the days went by we saw several unusual things at the checkpoint. On March 1, 1991 as I was standing my shift at the checkpoint we were notified that Iraqi soldiers in uniform would be passing through our checkpoint in a few minutes. We were to let them pass without stopping them. They were traveling toward Safwan to sign the cease-fire agreement with General Schwarzkopf. Shortly two SUV's came from the west at high speed, slowing only momentarily as they passed us. I felt like shouting at them about the atrocities committed by their army in Kuwait, but I was more curious to see what they looked like than vent any anger. In the end, I really didn't get to see much. The vehicle was just a blur as they passed on their mission to deceive General Schwarzkopf about the use of their helicopters. They returned through the checkpoint later that day after my shift was over. It is disconcerting to think I was so close to these thugs and yet not able to do anything to stop them from doing even more evil in their own country.

Another of the most bizarre things I saw was an old man with three goats. It had been a slow morning at the checkpoint. It was well past mid morning. In the distance to the west we saw what looked like an old man with three goats. We had seen sheep all over the Middle East, but not many goats. And these were not even average size goats. These looked like pygmy goats. They had long, floppy ears, big eyes and fluffy tails. We knew what lay behind us. There was nothing for many, many miles. Over the previous few days we had seen many types of vehicles from huge grain trucks to the smallest of cars, but we had never seen anyone on foot.

Almost every vehicle we had seen was loaded with the possessions of the people driving the car or truck. The only thing this old man had was a stick to control his goats. As he drew closer we could see him in more detail. He had a long white beard and wore a white robe and turban. The turban seemed out of place since most of the men we had seen wore the traditional head covering of the Arabs. His legs were partly exposed because he had tucked part of his robe into a waistband. The robe seemed more like something I had seen people from India wear than those of the Middle East. His skin was very dark and wrinkled from much exposure to the sun. He was very thin and a short little fellow of about four and a half feet tall.

As he approached we could tell that he had no weapons. It would be pointless to search him. I wondered how many miles he had walked that morning. I wondered how he would eat and how he would get water for himself and his goats. One of the men grabbed an MRE and a small bottle of water and held it out as he passed by. He kept staring strait ahead, seemingly oblivious to the fact that we were even there. He never missed a stride. He just kept walking like he had been doing it all his life, never stopping to eat, sleep or drink. I stared in awe as I watched him pass by. It was like a miniature parade, a mirage we had all dreamed up in our imagination.

As I saw his small figure and those of his goats get lost in the shimmering mirage of the heat irradiating off of the blacktop headed east I wondered about his history. What had happened in his life that had made him walk that road? I wondered if he had a future. We had all been concerned when we saw Iraqis carrying everything they owned on the back of a truck. This man had less than that. He had no visible family, no livelihood except the three goats, and no possessions to speak of. He didn't even have food or water to sustain him and was so oblivious to us that he hadn't accepted our generosity. Yet, even with all these detractors, his thin elderly frame never missed a beat. It is scenes like this that I will never forget from my time in the Middle East. It makes you realize that as an American, even on the worst day of our lives, most of us have a better future than this little man.

On another occasion, a little white car crammed full of people of all ages, approached our checkpoint from the west. On top of the car was a simple wooden casket. This peaked our curiosity and made us wonder if it was a real casket or merely a ruse to sneak weapons past the checkpoint. As the soldiers on duty approached the car it stopped short of the checkpoint. As it came to a halt a distressed woman opened the car door and approached them. The interpreter stepped forward and began listening to the woman. He talked with her for a couple of minutes and told the soldiers to let them go without searching the car. The distress of the woman was palpable and real. The interpreter could smell the stench of a rotting corpse. I was a stickler for following orders, but even I agreed that this one should go without a search.

We had found nothing since we had been assigned to the checkpoint. It was doubtful the car carried any weapons. I rationalized that anyone who would put up with that stench in order to smuggle weapons into Basra probably wasn't with the Iraqi Army. I wouldn't mind a few weapons from the other side getting through if the coffin did hold weapons. They were opposing Sadam Hussein. Anyone who did that had my vote. The family headed down the road toward Basra to bury their loved one. The body was well past due to go into the ground. The heat of the day made it even more urgent.

Later that evening at dusk the car returned. The casket was still there. The smell was even worse. The interpreter told us the Republican Guard had set up a checkpoint outside the city and refused them entrance into the city. This time they were in even more distress. The driver, a middle-aged man, got out of the car this time as well as three women. The interpreter talked with them and motioned them to go back the way they had come originally. It was obvious they didn't want to do that. Eventually they did as he directed.

The interpreter told us that according to family and religious tradition their family was supposed to be buried in a certain cemetery. It would be a complete disaster to have the family member buried somewhere else. The interpreter finally convinced the family that the corpse needed to go into the ground quickly or it would be an even greater disgrace for the family. He suggested to the family to bury the corpse in a temporary place until the situation changed. They reluctantly agreed. As they drove off down the road I was reminded how religious and family traditions, as wonderful as they are in peaceful times, can become a hugely distressing thing in troubled times.

One evening a white Toyota pickup was stopped. In the cab were a large Arab man and two women. In the bed were another woman and several small children. The guard asked the people to step out as another searched the truck. Once completed, everyone got back in the truck except the man. We could tell that the women and children were hungry. We saw no food in the truck. One of the guards tore open an MRE and began handing food to the children.

The large Arab man with the protruding waistline stopped the guard and motioned that he should get the food, not the children. The guard ignored the man and tried again to give food to the children. As this was happening the youngest woman, who was very pretty, walked around the side of the truck and began talking with the man in an excited manner. The other guard reached out with some food for the young woman and the large Arab man snatched it out of the guards' hand. Then the pretty young woman did something that shocked and delighted me. She took her right hand and swung it at his face. The man obviously was not prepared for her to take a swing at him. His head jolted as her hand hit his jaw.

A shocked expression came over his face as she took the food out of the mans' hand. Suddenly he lunged at the young woman to recover the food. As he did one of my men stepped in front of the man and put his M16 across his chest to keep him from moving. The man was now upset with us as well as the woman. As he motioned to push the guard away the other guard chambered a round and pointed the weapon in his direction. The man was suddenly placid. As I gave food to the children and women everyone else was transfixed in place. The children tore open the packets of food and began to eat. The women looked at me with thankful eyes and mouthed words I didn't understand.

Once the young woman was back in the pickup we gave the man some food and he got back in his pickup. Loud talking could be heard coming from the cab of the pickup as the man yelled at the younger woman and she yelled back. The two other women also added their voices to the fray. Finally the man glared at us through the closed window of the little white pickup and drove toward Basra. I was curious to know what the women had said to the man. I could take a pretty good guess. I knew what American women would have said to this man. But this was not America and these were not American women. This culture was very different from our own. I wondered if the women, especially the young woman, would suffer reprisals. I wondered if the children would too. For a woman to strike a man in this culture, especially this man, who knew what the consequences would be? I had seen just how brutal men could be to women in this culture when we visited the villages with the medics.

One of the best things that happened at the checkpoint was when a bus arrived heading toward Basra. As the Bus emptied itself of its passengers, I groaned at the thought of searching so many people. I decided to search a few people myself so that my soldiers could get a break and watch the crowd. After I had searched several I got a tap on my shoulder from one of my men, asking if he could take over. I was grateful. I walked over to the side of the road just in time to see the last of the bus riders step down the steps. The black, brown and navy blue burkas (Islamic women's robes which cover head to toe) mixed with the white men's robes in the sea of people. I looked back at the door of the bus just as the last woman stepped down. I was stunned. Before me was a beautiful young woman in sky blue and white robes with a gold necklace. As she looked at me she smiled. Perfect white teeth illuminated a beautiful face. Since Kathy, no woman had smiled at me. She was a vision.

Most Arab women are afraid to smile at a man for fear of the men in their family. This woman was definitely traveling alone and very self-confident. She held her head confidently, moving with grace among the sea of the repressed. I couldn't take my eyes off her. I hadn't seen anything this beautiful in months. "Hello", she said. I was delighted, but startled. She actually spoke English! I couldn't believe it. I asked her where she learned English. She said that she had lived in the United States for three years while attending college. She was going back to visit her parents in Basra before returning to finish college. I wished her good luck and she wished me the same.

The whole encounter gave me a lift in spirit and hope for the future. I wanted desperately to find out her name, her address, her phone number. But I put this aside as I realized the situation. I knew knowing her better would only complicate both our lives. But seeing her for just a few minutes was like finding a blue gemstone in the vastness of the desert.

The most troubling thing I saw at the checkpoint happened as the Republican Guard was attacking the city of Basra. I had seen many people in the last few days heading for Basra. I wondered how these people were faring now that the city was being bombed by helicopters and attacked on the ground by remnants of the Republican Guard. For several evenings, after the majority of traffic had died down, we watched about sixty miles eastward toward the city of Basra. After dark we could clearly see and hear bombs dropping on the city. There was the low thud, thud as the bombs exploded a while after we had seen the flashes. It seemed like we were selling out the people of Basra. We had just defeated a huge part of the Iraqi Army, and now the remainder of that army was pounding the city of Basra. Why couldn't we do anything? It felt frustrating.

Intellectually I knew our mission was over. However, I also knew that it wouldn't take much for us to move in and keep the Iraqi Army from killing the people of Basra. Just a show of force on our part would have made them run. As a minimum our air defense units, our air force or our helicopter gun ships could shoot down a few Iraqi helicopters. These helicopters were violating the spirit of the cease-fire agreement we had signed with the Iraqis.

As we were talking about these very issues we could see headlights in the distance coming toward the checkpoint from Basra. As the vehicle drew nearer it slowed to a stop on the side of the road a little distance from the checkpoint. It was a little white truck with several people in the front and back. The driver, an Arab man, and an Arab woman who had come from the passenger side quickly approached the interpreter, who was walking toward them. As the woman reached the interpreter she fell to her knees and put her head on his feet, weeping profusely.

The man stopped short and began to tell the interpreter what was happening. While the man and the interpreter talked the woman wailed. She shook her head from side to side in a most pitiful way, from time to time grabbing the interpreters' legs and pulling her head into them. The Arab man became more animated as he talked and began to sob as well, finally wiping his reddened eyes with his sleeve. When the man was finished telling his story the interpreter took a second and breathed a deep sigh. He looked back at us briefly, and then began to talk quietly, slowly to the couple.

After several minutes the sobbing died down and the interpreter shook his head. The sobbing man finally picked up the woman and walked her back to the pickup. As the pickup made a U-turn and headed back to Basra, its red taillights getting smaller in the distance, the interpreter told us what the couple had said. Soldiers from the Iraqi Army had broken down the door of their house, forced their way inside, and abducted their teenage daughter. They were pleading with us to go and rescue their only daughter. The interpreter told them there was nothing we could do. Then the Kuwaiti interpreter said a startling thing, "That is what they get for letting Sadam Hussein run their country." Understandably he was very upset with what Sadam had done to his country. Two of his family members had been murdered during the invasion of Kuwait.

That night I couldn't get what was happening to the people of Basra out of my head. As the thud, thud of the bombs exploded over Basra I wondered if there was anything I could do. To be this close with a conquering military force and be forced to sit and watch helplessly as the people of Basra were maimed, murdered and raped was unconscionable. We had just liberated Kuwait from this same army. Why were we not being allowed to do the same for these people? The Third Armored Division sat as Basra cried for help.

In my dreams I fantasized about doing the only thing I could do. I somehow convinced my crew that going into Basra and fighting the Iraqi army was the right thing to do. As we headed toward Basra and certain death or imprisonment if we survived the radio crackled for us to stop and turn around. As we raced toward Basra word of our insanity reached higher headquarters and a tank platoon was ordered to bring us back.

As this tank platoon moved into the zone between the coalition army and the Iraqis, the Iraqis opened fire on the American tanks. The American tanks opened fire on the Iraqis, destroying them. The Iraqi commander contacted the commander of the forces attacking Basra and informed him that the Third Armored Division was attacking. As my Bradley approached the Basra city limits, the Iraqi army was in full retreat heading back toward Baghdad.

Instantaneously, my crew and I were riding in a convertible in a ticker tape parade down Fifth Avenue in New York City. Then I woke up to the cold, dark reality of the hell the people of Basra were suffering and the cowardice of both the President and me.

20

The Donkey Incident

After a week and a half of working this checkpoint nonstop we were all exhausted. We had seen tankers come and go several times. All they had to do was sit in their tanks and scan the area to their front. Yet they had been relieved every two days and we hadn't. One evening I was at the checkpoint watching the city of Basra get bombed another time when the Battalion Commander arrived in his Humvee. He asked how we were doing.

Normally I would have just told a high-ranking officer "Fine". It was pointless to usurp the chain of command unless there was something the lower ranking officers had been unable to handle. I figured this was one of those times. Since he had been concerned enough to brief us personally before we crossed into Iraq, I figured I had a better chance of getting something done by talking to him. Besides, my platoon leader and company commander were no longer in my chain of command while I was on this checkpoint. So I spoke up and told him that my men and I were getting worn out.

With only ten men working 24/7 searching vehicles and people we needed a break. I asked him to put another unit on the checkpoint for just a day so that we could have some downtime. He said that he didn't have anyone else who could do the job. I asked him to please tell me when we would get relieved so that my men would have something to look forward to. He said he didn't know and rode away.

I felt betrayed. I felt like no one cared. There was no end in sight. The next morning I switched to the platoon frequency and called LT Wynn. He also gave me no hope. There was no word how long we would be there. There was no one to relieve us. Even though we were all together, my section could not even get together and let off steam. We were either monitoring the radio, working the checkpoint, eating or sleeping. One day melted into another. Time meant nothing except that it was your time on the checkpoint.

During this time wild dogs roamed the desert looking for food in large packs of twenty or thirty animals. The command thought it a concern and sent higher-ranking NCOs to run them off or kill them. When these NCOs came to our area the dogs fled. One of the NCOs told me that I could kill them, too if they came in our area. A couple days later a small group of five came into our area. I walked toward them waving my arms and all of them ran except one. I loaded a round into my .45 and aimed it at the dogs' head. The dog cowered under me. I couldn't bring myself to kill it. This dog didn't seem like a threat. It was just scared. I put a round in the sand behind its tail and it ran away. I hoped they wouldn't come again.

One afternoon I was awakened from a sweaty nap by one of my crew. A herd of about twenty donkeys was approaching our checkpoint from the north. My crew thought this to be a curious oddity and figured I would want to see it if for nothing else than to relieve the boredom. I was still half-asleep and not amused. I watched as the herd headed for the spot where chow was delivered for the morning and evening meals, just across the road from my Bradley. They began to sniff the ground and eat any scraps that happened to be on the ground. The Army had taught us to keep the area where we ate as clean as possible and there wasn't much there in the way of scraps. The lead donkey looked up and began to move the herd in my direction.

The ramp was down on the Bradley with a trash bag containing the remnants of the breakfast and lunch meals hanging in plain sight. Our tent was open and another trash bag hung in the doorway. They were headed for the trash bags. I knew if I let them get near the Bradley or the tent they would make a mess and be a constant menace thereafter. I had only seen wild donkeys once before near Cripple Creek, Colorado. The locals there warned visitors not to go near them, that they could be dangerous. Their kick had been known to kill a man and they were known for biting people. I wanted to discourage these intruders from being there and coming back.

I waved my arms and yelled. The donkeys stopped and starred at me for a second then began to move toward the trash bags again. I waved my arms again and yelled a little louder, moving toward them as I did. As I moved toward them it was clear they didn't want to move. I pulled out my 45-caliber pistol and chambered a round. I wasn't about to let these animals have the run of the place, and I wanted to have something to stop them if they got aggressive. I waved my arms again, yelled even louder and began to run toward them. This turned the herd around and they began moving off in the opposite direction. I kept walking behind them as they moved back north. Every time I slowed down the herd would stop and begin to turn around. I fired a round into the sand behind them, hoping the sound would motivate them to move. As I did, the sound was muffled from the wind blowing to the east.

I waived my arms and yelled as loud as I could, moving toward them in an aggressive way. They began to move again. As they neared the farthest limits of the line of tanks I heard a tanker yell something, but the wind muffled the sound. The tanks were about one quarter mile away. I ran at the donkeys again and fired two quick rounds into the sand behind them. This didn't seem to have any effect on them, but they kept moving. As I walked back to my tent to get some more sleep I suddenly felt like I was wearing lead boots. The tanker platoon sergeant ran over to me and began yelling at me. Why had I fired those rounds? Was there Iraqis in the area?

I told him, no, I was just scaring some donkeys out of the area. He yelled that I could have hit some of his men. I told him there was no way I could have hit any of his men since I fired into the sand. I told him I could find the bullets if he wanted. He seemed disgusted and walked quickly out of the tent. In a few minutes the tanker platoon leader came in the tent and woke me up. He wanted me to repeat what I had told the platoon sergeant. I did and then asked him to please let me get some rest.

He seemed a little more sympathetic, but in about forty-five minutes a humvee pulled up with the Mortar Platoon Sergeant, SFC Montgomery, inside. The platoon leader told me that I would need to go with Sergeant Montgomery. He would be taking me to the medics. They took my pistol and gave it to SGT Beets. I wasn't in any condition to argue. My mind was now as fuzzy as a bag of cotton balls. I was so tired I could hardly make it to the humvee.

As we rode along, the desert seemed blurry. I tried to rest but the bumpy ride of the humvee didn't allow it. SFC Montgomery wanted to know what had happened. I weakly told him what I knew. He said he had heard I had tried to kill someone. I suddenly wasn't tired anymore. I told him in no uncertain terms that it was the farthest thing from the truth. I told him again what had happened and emphasized the fact that there was no one even close to me when I fired, that I had fired into the ground away from any soldiers. He seemed to be satisfied with that and told me to calm down and get some rest. I immediately felt tired down to my toes.

The next thing I knew I was being helped out of the humvee and led into a tent. I was put into a chair and asked to wait. I wanted to tell the person I didn't have the strength to move, but couldn't form the words. The next thing I remember is answering questions about the incident from someone I had never seen before. They wore an officer's uniform with a medical insignia. I saw books on psychiatry. A shrink was interviewing me.

"Great!" I thought. Not only do some people think I tried to kill someone, but now some people think I'm crazy! I told the shrink the same thing I had told everyone else. The shrink kept asking me about firing the weapon in the air. I repeated the fact that I had not fired into the air; I had fired into the ground in front of me. There was no possibility that anyone would have been in danger. It seemed like the whole world was against me. Didn't anyone understand that I was only trying to control a situation before it got out of control?

The last thing I wanted was for one of my men to get bitten or kicked by one of these large animals. I didn't want my men interrupted by wild animals wandering through the area while they were trying to search vehicles or get some rest. Who knew what would happen if the donkeys were in the area when the hot food arrived? Would they aggressively attack the food servers? The vast desert had little to eat. A famished wild animal could do just about anything. A herd of them could do a lot of damage.

I was taken to a medic tent where I was put on an elevated stretcher and given two bags of saline solution to relieve dehydration. I slept while this was being done, waking briefly while they changed bags. After this was done I stood up and felt the color come back to my face. I felt a little wobbly, so I was helped to a folding chair in the corner. After a few minutes I told the medics I felt better. I stood up and felt good legs under me. I still felt a little weak, but when asked if I could make it to the chow tent I readily said "yes".

I was escorted over to the chow tent by a young woman soldier who helped me fill my tray. After finding a place to sit she said she would be back in a few minutes to show me to a tent where I would spend the night. As I slowly ate a bland army meal I wondered what lay in store for me. Would my platoon now think I was a nut? My weapon had been taken; would I get it back? Would charges be forthcoming? I would be in lockup right now if that were the case, I figured. Would I get to go back to my platoon or spend the rest of the deployment in a hospital? I wondered how things could have spun so out of control.

The woman soldier returned after about twenty minutes. I was just finishing my meal. She sat down across from me and told me that the nurse would be giving me a shot to help me sleep. I wanted to tell her that it wouldn't be necessary. I felt like I could sleep a couple of days. I was given a shot inside a very well lit tent and a blanket for the nights stay. I was told that someone from my platoon would be picking me up in the morning. It was recommended that I get comfortable right away since the shot would take effect in a few minutes. I was shown a dark tent where army cots where packed from one end of the tent to the other on both sides. I stowed my helmet, LBE and boots under a cot and made my protective mask case into a pillow. I lay down and pulled the blanket over me.

As I lay there in the darkness I could here two soldiers, a man and a woman, whispering. The young man wanted to know if she was seeing another man. She told him no and wanted him to be quiet. He wanted to press the issue. He accused her of having sex with a guy named Tom. She remained silent. "Aha!" he said with an accusatorial air. "Then you are having sex with him!" he said. "No," came the reply from the young woman. "I just don't want to have sex with *you* any more."

He was silent for a few seconds. I began to doze off. As I drifted off to sleep I could here him saying, "What is it? Do I need a new technique? I can do something different, you know." I wondered how the combat soldiers could have it so different from the rest of the army. My men were suffering while the rest of the army was bickering over sexual partners.

The next morning I got up and, after a shower and shave, I got in line for breakfast. I had forgotten how hot scrambled eggs could be when they were cooked in front of you. There was no green tint to them either. The bacon was crisp. The mermite cans sometimes made bacon have the consistency of beef jerky. Even the coffee was hotter. I burnt my lips on the first sip I tried. I took an ice cube from the iced fruit display and put it in my cup. After the ice cube melted it was just about right. We hadn't seen ice since before the war started. I walked back to the tent and sat on the cot. I felt a lot better after a good night's rest and a very hot breakfast.

I felt out of place. Almost everyone in the area was wearing desert camouflage BDU's (Battle Dress Uniform). Even some civilian personnel were walking around in them. You could easily tell them from soldiers. They didn't wear any rank, nametags or unit patches. Their demeanor was different. They walked differently, talked differently and even acted differently. They didn't have any military bearing. They didn't use military courtesy or address anyone by rank. It goaded me that these people had desert camouflage BDU's and we combat soldiers on the front lines still didn't have any. It seemed like we were the redheaded stepchildren of the army.

One of the medics came in the tent and called my name. I rose and went over to him. He gave me some pills in a paper envelope with written instructions on the front. I was to take two pills every twenty-four hours, beginning when I arrived back at the platoon area. Someone from my troop would be there shortly to take me back. I was to wait in the tent until they arrived. I put my helmet on the far end of the cot and propped my protective mask on it at an angle to give my head some elevation while I waited. I wondered what the men of my platoon were thinking. At least I wasn't handcuffed, I thought.

I still felt tired and weak. As I lay there I couldn't help listening to the petty problems the people in the tent were having. One was complaining that the mess tent had run out of butter. Another was complaining that the barber hadn't cut his hair right. Still another complained that he had to stand guard for an hour the previous night. I wanted to scream for all of them to shut up. I wanted to tell them that we rarely got butter with our meals, hadn't had a haircut in weeks and my men stood guard on a checkpoint several times a day for much longer than one hour. I wanted to tell them that they didn't know hardship. I wanted to tell them they couldn't handle hardship. I wanted to tell them that any one of my men was better than any three of theirs. I wanted to, but I didn't. I bit my lip and secretly prayed my ride would be there quickly.

A few minutes later someone called my name and said my ride was there. I put on my gear and walked outside. There I saw the 1SG's driver with his humvee. I climbed in the passenger seat and tried to get comfortable. The driver said he had one more stop to make before we headed back to the company area. He drove over to another tent on the far side of the assembly area and parked. I told him I would wait until he was finished. He wasn't gone long.

He returned to the humvee with a chocolate cake wrapped in aluminum foil. He asked me to hold it while we went over some rough roads getting back to the blacktop. The bakery was now in full operation. We would be getting fresh rolls and baked goods from now on. He was right; we would be getting these things. However, rolls always seem better when they are still hot from the oven rather than pulled from inside a plastic garbage bag several hours later. Cakes rarely held together after they had bumped along on those desert trails. Instead of a nice slice of cake, most of us got a mountain of crumbs with frosting mixed in.

When we arrived at the platoon area I was dropped off at SFC Z's tent. I told him what the medics had said and showed him the tablets I had been given. I took a slug of water from my canteen and washed the tablets down. The paper the medics had given me said I was on bed rest for 2 days. Sergeant Z pointed me to a cot and told me to get some rest. He didn't ask me about the incident or lecture me about anything.

Within just a few minutes I was out. I drifted in and out of consciousness for several hours. From time to time I could here platoon members talking in the tent. They discussed the incident as though I wasn't there. They generally seemed confused by what I had done but not judgmental. It was late morning the next day when I woke up. I got something to eat, took my pills and went back to sleep. Someone woke me when breakfast arrived the next day. I stood in line and got some semi-hot chow.

The green tinged eggs had returned. Sergeant Z briefed me that my section was now in a different location. Sergeant Ferillo's section had been swapped with mine. We were now guarding the main highway from Basra to Baghdad, Highway Eight. This was a four-lane road running generally parallel with the other road. We were no longer searching people, just vehicles. Traffic was half what it had been on the other road. Tanks blocked the road and slowed traffic to a crawl before it reached my men. The loader and driver on the tanks were now tasked to help us search vehicles. If trouble happened it was a short hop to get back on their tanks.

The new rotation for checkpoint duty now allowed my section to relax a little more. I hitched a ride with the chow crew to get to my Bradley. As I climbed out of the humvee I spotted my Bradley and slowly walked over to it. SGT Beets was in the turret and climbed down just as I approached. The others had gone to eat. SGT Beets smiled at me and asked me if I was rested. I told him I was. He asked me what it was like in the rear area. Did I see any women back there? I told him I had, but none of them were very good looking.

He laughed and said any woman would look good to him. As we talked I was relieved that he was making me feel like a part of the team again. He made it feel like I had just been on vacation and was envious. I told him that even civilians were walking around in desert camouflage. He rolled his eyes and asked me to tell him more. I told him all I had seen. He was as floored as I. The rest of the crew returned from chow. They all said "hi, Sergeant Abbott" between slurps of milk and bites of food. They ribbed me about taking a couple of days off.

SGT Beets slid out of the back of the Bradley and strapped on his gear. He asked me if I had eaten. I said yes, but I would walk with him to get chow. He said OK, then stopped, turned around and reached back inside the turret. "Here", he said, "You may need this." He stuck my shoulder holster containing my 45-caliber pistol toward me. I took it from his large hand and casually strapped it on as we walked toward the chow line. That gesture was what I needed to feel like I had come full circle. It was the ultimate gesture of trust. It was a gesture of understanding from a man who knew what it was like to walk in my shoes.

21

The Camel Steaks

After we moved back to a position inside Kuwait life got a little better. We assembled our platoon with the mortar platoon in a fighting position that looked like a star when viewed from above. The Bradleys were at the tip of each star point facing out with the mortar tracks on the inside points of the star. After we had positioned our vehicles the commander sent an engineer vehicle, which resembled a small bulldozer, to push up the sand around the edges to the height of about four feet. On top of this we wound a single strand of concertina wire, staked down to the sand berm so that the wind wouldn't blow it down.

We were told that tomorrow evening we would be getting a steak dinner, provided by the Kuwaitis. Steak! None of us had had a steak in months. The thought of a juicy steak was constant in our thoughts. We wrote letters home about it. We dreamed about the experience as we drifted off to sleep that night. The war was over and we were appreciated for the work we had done. Finally someone was recognizing combat soldiers.

Some of us had seen how the rear echelon soldiers lived. Someone had read a copy of the Stars and Stripes newspaper where several Air Force personnel had been hospitalized for respiratory problems. The stress of going from air-conditioned tents to the hot, dry desert air had hurt their lungs. We didn't feel sorry for them. We were shocked.

We assumed that all of the military would be living in the same conditions. None of us had been under air conditioning since our stay at Al Kobar towers. Even then, the temperature was set so high it didn't seem like it was on at all. To think that there were military personnel in this desert who had the temperature set so low as to cause lung problems from the extreme variation in temperature and humidity was unthinkable. It made us sick to think how the other half lived.

They were probably sick of steak. We were just about to get our first one in months.

We were all in good spirits the next morning. Men were smiling who hadn't smiled in days. We ate the same breakfast we had gotten used to again, but it didn't matter. We smiled and joked as the green-tinged eggs were spooned onto our paper plates. Even the lukewarm milk didn't bother us. We had visions of thick, juicy, succulent steak dancing before us. We asked the soldiers who brought us our food and mail if they had white tablecloths on which to serve the steak? No, they said, but the cooks were adding something special: baked potatoes with sour cream, butter, salt and pepper. They were also adding fresh salad with dressing, dinner rolls and even A-1 steak sauce for the steaks.

The smiles grew into pure joy. How could we be so lucky? Yes, we were stuck in the desert while unit after unit redeployed to the United States. Yes, we wondered when we would ever see our families again. But at least we were going to have a steak dinner tonight, something to take our minds off home. We were going to feast like kings! As the time for the evening meal grew closer, each of us were anxious to see the steak dinner unloaded. I grabbed a well-used copy of the Stars and Stripes and began to read to make the time go quickly. After each article I would look up to see if I could see the plume of dust which would be coming down the road announcing the arrival of the evening feast.

I finished all of the articles that interested me and, seeing no dust plume, I began reading articles that were only slightly interesting. Finishing these articles, I began to reread the first articles. After the second article I heard someone shout, "Chow is here!" No one had to search for soldiers to let them know the steaks had arrived. Soldiers from every point of the star began converging on the truck hauling the precious meal. Volunteers suddenly began to help unloading the truck without being asked. I took a deep breath of air through my nose to see if I could smell the steak. I could smell nothing. Of course, I thought, they were sealed inside the food cans. The food line formed quickly.

Good NCOs (Noncommissioned officers) and officers always let their men eat first to insure that they were fed before they permit themselves to eat. This is good for morale and shows the soldiers that their Officers and NCOs are concerned about them. One of my soldiers joked that they hadn't brought enough steaks for the officers and NCOs. Ha, ha I thought. I smiled and feigned laughter. One of the officers said they hoped the cooks could count. As we stood in line holding our paper plates we could see the steaks coming out of the food cans. I was puzzled by what I saw.

These steaks didn't look like any steak I had ever seen. The color was a brownish gray with a knot of fat on one side. The sides were curled up so that the steak looked more like a bowl than a piece of steak. As I inhaled through my nose to capture the aroma, I was surprised to not find any. There was a slight hint of something that had been put to the flame, but it didn't really smell like anything in my memory. I kept thinking to myself, well, it's the taste that is the important thing. Just wait until you bite into that steak. How it smells will not be important.

After receiving my steak and a huge baked potato, I piled some huge leaves of lettuce with large slices of tomato on my plate. I piled high the condiments on top of my huge baked potato wrapped in foil. It was smothered in sour cream and butter. I passed on the A-1 sauce. I wanted to taste the steak. I shuffled over to a stack of MRE cases and sat down. I was in my own little world.

The steak glistened before me. I wanted to eat it before it got cold. I tried to mix my baked potato together with the butter and sour cream so they would be melting together while I began eating my steak. I couldn't. The baked potato was warm, but it was as hard as a rock; obviously it had been undercooked. Crestfallen, I looked at my steak and began to cut a piece with my plastic knife. The knife only scratched the surface even after many swipes of the knife. I reluctantly pulled my pocketknife and began to cut in the same place I had tried with my plastic knife.

I forced the knife so hard on the paper plate that my corn began to spill over the side. I steadied my plate on my legs, picked up the steak with my left hand and my fingers on either side of the partial cut, which had been made in the piece of meat. I was determined to get a piece cut off. With my right hand I took the knife and ran it down the groove in the meat over and over again until it was almost severed from the main piece of meat. A tough little piece still kept the meat in one piece. I hacked at this piece over and over again until it finally gave way to my knife. The little bite-sized piece fell to my plate and almost fell into the sand.

I breathed a sigh of relief, picked up the piece of meat and placed it in my mouth. As I began to chew, I welcomed the flavor of this steak. It didn't come. It tasted as bland as it had smelled. Yet, I was determined to eat this steak. The more I chewed, the more I tried to enjoy it. I chewed and chewed and chewed. The longer I chewed the bigger this piece of meat grew. I couldn't chew a piece small enough to swallow. It all stayed in one piece. I finally had to spit it out. Still determined, I took the main portion of the steak in both hands and chomped down on it as hard as I could.

My teeth were stuck in the steak. I shook my head to try and tear the piece out. I suddenly became self-conscious of my actions. I was sure someone had noticed that I was eating like a dog. I cautiously looked around to see if anyone had spotted me in this ridiculous situation. All I could see were soldiers having the same trouble I was having and doing the same thing. Grumbling could be heard from every corner. Soldiers began to say things like, "Does anyone have a sharp knife?" "This steak is as tough as leather!", and "What kind of steak is this anyway?"

I munched on a leaf of lettuce while I decided what I was going to do next. What could I do? The steak was like leather. How could I eat it if I couldn't even chew a bite-sized piece? As I sat pondering my dilemma I watched others around me to see what they were doing. Inside our area we had a huge pit dug to burn trash. Soldier after soldier filed past this pit and reluctantly dropped the evening meal into it. I resigned myself to the same fate and did the same thing.

Looking down into the pit at the numerous pieces of meat with gnawed teeth marks on them, I could only think of what a waste this meal had been. I didn't make eye contact with anyone. I just slowly walked back to my Bradley, which had the ramp resting on an ammo box, and sat down on the ramp. What now? I was still hungry. I reluctantly pulled out a case of MREs and opened it. Inside were all the MREs the other soldiers on my crew didn't like, which I had been eating since we had left Al Kobar Towers. I opened some crackers and smeared them with peanut butter.

As I pondered the meaning of what had just happened I felt like spitting nails at someone. The one thing we had looked forward to had ended in disgrace. The Stars and Stripes no longer mentioned welcoming anyone home from the Gulf. Life had returned to normal in the States and we were still stuck in the Middle

East. I tried not to feel sorry for my self, but the disgrace was just more than I could stand. As the sun set on the vast desert I crawled into my sleeping bag and dreamed of the day I could sit down in a real restaurant with a beautiful woman and a decent steak.

22

The Oil Fires

Before we could deploy back to Germany we needed to offload our ammunition. In the past we had always offloaded ammunition by counting, cleaning and repackaging. Then we would turn in the ammunition to the ammunition handlers for storage or shipment to another secure location. This time it would be different. We were given a map route and the location of a live fire range in southeastern Kuwait. We weren't turning in this ammunition we were going to fire all of it, except for most of the TOW rounds. Each Bradley would get to fire two; the ones already stored in the launcher. The rest would be checked for damage including a check of the humidity indicator. Any damaged missiles would be destroyed by EOD.

On the morning of the live fire range we packed everything except the camouflage nets into the Bradleys and got in line outside of the assembly area. We would be firing some of the ammo at night and would not be returning until the next day. The mortar platoon was left behind to provide security for the area while we were gone. They would fire their ammo with another unit after we returned. As we moved out it felt good to be on the move again. I felt conflicted, however, about the firing of these rounds.

My whole Army career it had been emphasized that this was expensive ammunition. Many times our training had been canceled or abbreviated for lack of money for ammunition. Simulators had been bought by the Army to save money on ammunition and fuel. Every round we fired had to be accounted for and any ammunition not fired had to be turned in. None of us had ever fired a live anti-tank missile with a real warhead. I had fired two TOW missiles; both had been training rounds without a warhead. Now we were going to fire two types of anti-tank missiles, all of the 25mm main gun rounds, all of the M16 and M1911 (pistol) rounds, all of the M203 grenade launcher rounds and all of the M249 coax rounds.

This was more than I had probably fired my whole career. I knew it would be good training for all of us, but it seemed like such a waste. The war was over. Some of these men were getting out of the Army. Our unit was being deactivated. It just seemed more logical and frugal to give this ammo to another unit for use with their next training cycle. Even the tanks were firing all of their rounds. I was told that the whole Third Armored Division was doing the same thing. The amount of ammunition to be fired would be in the hundreds of thousands of dollars. We would have fun, but it seemed such a waste.

As we moved along down the desert trail running parallel to some large power lines I could tell we were going to be passing by the Kuwaiti oil fires. The wind was blowing to the south that day, toward Saudi Arabia. The thick black plumes of smoke billowed up then to the right leaving a crystal blue sky above and a hazy dark gray smudge beneath. I wondered how we would be able to breathe when we passed by this inferno. The closer we approached the better we could see the flames. They weren't like any flames I had ever seen.

Giant pillars of intense red shot into the air like a stream from a fire hose. Flickers of brilliant yellow and vibrant orange punctuated the pillars like small explosions on the sun. The fires seemed placed like the candles on a birthday cake, unnatural and surreal. Immediately above the burning flames were the towers of dense, thick, impenetrable black smoke being shot high into the air. It struck me as such a waste. How many homes could've been heated this winter by this burning oil? How many miles could be driven from the gasoline? How many lives would have been enriched had these fires not been set?

As we drew closer I could tell we would have no problem breathing. There was a huge gap between the earth and the smoke cloud being generated by the oil fires. As we drove under the thick black cloud the sun looked like a silver disk hanging in the sky. From time to time it would change color to a light yellow. It reminded me of a passage from the Bible that talked of the sun changing color.

The firing range was just beyond the oil fires, between the fires and the Persian Gulf. A few destroyed vehicles as well as some cardboard silhouettes had been placed on the range for targets. A road had to be blocked at each end that ran behind the range. We were only allowed to fire at certain times. Between these times traffic would be allowed to travel down this road. We were *not* allowed to fire at moving targets. There were none. Any moving targets spotted during firing would initiate a cease-fire. We fired all of our rounds in day and night firings. Afterward, it was just a matter of policing the brass and cleaning the weapons.

23

Movie Night

Ever since the camel steaks fiasco I felt depressed and claustrophobic. Even though we were in a huge desert, we hadn't been allowed to go anywhere and had no real mission. We were basically waiting for our time to turn in our vehicles and fly back to Germany. Most of us just fell into a funk. We walked around like zombies much of the time. But some of the guys had a much harder time than I. One soldier only received one letter from his parents the whole time we were in the Middle East. The letter reminded him that they had opposed his joining the army and basically said, "You've dug your own grave." It is stories like this that seldom get told. Most people think everyone's family supports them in a time of war. It just isn't true. This soldier and a few others began to burn themselves with cigarettes and make very crude tattoos using razor blades, needles from the medics bag and blue ink. We felt as though we had been left in the desert to rot.

Of course there were the times when the monotony was broken. The battalion rotated a television set with a VCR and a portable generator among the assembly areas after the war. When we heard the rumor that we were going to watch TV for the first time since we left the port we were energized. But then, I wondered, how we would be able to get a signal so far into the desert? I put it out of my mind. I knew someone would have figured it out. We were told we would be getting the TV for one week and it would be arriving that afternoon. For American men who were accustomed to have TV most of their lives, this was more than a treat. This was like being in love with a beautiful woman.

A tent was erected in the middle of the assembly area and the sides were rolled up. When the truck arrived with the equipment there was no shortage of volunteers to help unload. In short order the equipment was ready and folding chairs were arranged in neat rows. Soldiers began to sit in the chairs, expecting to have the TV turned on immediately. The TV was tested to see that everything worked.

When it came on there was the familiar gray fuzz blanketing the screen. A small cheer went up to heaven accompanied by a few handclaps. There were smiles all around. Then came the announcement.

There was no TV reception. The first movie would be shown at 1800 hours (6 PM). "What movies do you have?" came the expected question. The soldier from battalion had a small box with VCR tapes inside. He reached inside and pulled out one after the other calling off their names as he did. "Which one would you like to see?" he said, once he was finished. The unanimous reply was "Lethal Weapon". The wait would be excruciating, but at least we had something to see. I walked back to my Bradley and pulled out pen and paper. Now I had something to write home about. It wasn't much, but anything was better than the crush of loneliness, isolation and letdown after the war.

The first night the tent was packed, with some soldiers standing at the back of the tent. It was surreal to be watching television in the middle of the desert at night. Occasionally I would take a quick peek outside the tent since the sides had been rolled and tied out of the way. The desert was void of lights and noise except for the light and sound from the television and the hum of the portable generator. This must be how it feels to be stranded on an ocean in a lifeboat with only a television to distract from the brutal reality of the situation, I thought.

The movie was great and a welcome distraction from the boredom of the camp. As the videos continued from best to worst the crowds began to dwindle as the days passed. All too soon, though, it was time to surrender this technology to another camp. Even though we had seen every video available worth watching, once the television was gone we all felt a little cheated. Boredom returned with a vengeance. We were back to drifting in an endless ocean of sand.

24

Presents For Orphans

Chaplain Kenehan came for a visit to our assembly area days later. He wasn't there to perform a service, he was just there to see if anyone needed to talk and gage our morale. I was nearby wanting to here any news from the outside world. As he spoke to Sergeant Z he made mention that he was going into Kuwait City today and wanted to know if he wanted to accompany him. He said that he didn't but asked me if I would like to go. Almost before he finished his sentence I said yes and asked the chaplain when he was leaving. He said in about five minutes. I told him I would be right back.

I nearly sprinted to my Bradley and told my crew where I was going, trying hard to conceal my excitement. I liked the chaplain. He was good company. The fact that I would be out of the desert and get to see some of the country we had just liberated was a huge plus. I climbed inside the humvee just as the chaplain was finishing. The chaplain said he was going into the city to visit an English speaking Christian mission. It was a place for the English speaking Christians to worship and had an orphanage. It wasn't exactly what I had hoped, but at least I was out of the assembly area.

As we rode along, the desert became monotonous. The scenery was the same as we had seen for months: endless sand, scattered piles of rocks, huge electrical towers. Just as I was putting my head down to rest a sight caught my eye. There in the near distance were huge piles of sand that had obviously been placed there. Placed there for what purpose, I wondered? Sticking out of the top of these piles I could see a large piece of metal pointing skyward. As we drew nearer I could tell it was the top of a large earth-moving machine. It was a sand and gravel pit.

Well, at least they sure had a big supply, but who would be stupid enough to buy sand in a desert? The chaplain pointed out the gravel pit and mentioned that the Kuwait road department owned the gravel pit. With all of the repairs that needed to be made on buildings and roads as well as new buildings being built they needed raw materials. Now it made sense. I put my head down and took a nap.

The humvee made a jerk and woke me from my nap. We were pulling into a small parking lot. I had missed the ride through the city. As I got out of the humvee I stretched my arms and legs. As I did Chaplain Kenehan and his driver, Specialist Sparks, walked to the back of the humvee and pulled out full trash bags. Chaplain Kenehan asked me to carry one.

There was a walled-in courtyard that had a small arched entrance with a metal gate swung open. As we walked toward the main building I wondered what was inside the bags. Then I remembered that a couple of weeks ago the chaplain had taken a collection to be used to buy toys for the orphans. Soldiers had given generously and now the orphans of this mission had toys to take their mind off their misery and dream of a better future. I was glad I was there. As we walked through the courtyard I noticed it was clean and shaded with several trees. Any shade was a much-welcomed relief from the blinding sun.

As we walked under the trees there was a noticeable drop in temperature. As Specialist Sparks swung the door open the chaplain walked into the large room with a big smile. Every face in the room now fixed on the chaplain, then all three of us. All at once there was a joyful rush as about twenty children from toddler to adolescent welcomed us. We couldn't help but be swept away in the joy of the moment. They didn't seem to notice the garbage bags; they wanted to see us! Two children hugged my legs as an older child hugged my waist. Others surrounded me and looked up with wanting eyes. The three of us were in a riotous sea of children.

I hugged the ones around me, kneeling down to get on their level. The shy ones just stood there watching, wanting to be a part of this welcome. I asked the ones around me to step back so I could say hi to the shy ones. Most obliged but one little one still clung to my leg. As I motioned to the shy ones to come on over they began to shuffle forward, stopped and ran back to the orphanage personnel. The director called to the children to move away from us and give us some breathing room. One young boy walked over to me, punched me in the arm and almost knocked me over. He ran away laughing gleefully. As I stood up I wondered if this was going to be a good experience.

That is when I saw him. Right next to the director of the orphanage was a young boy of about six who stood out like a wart on your nose. He was lively, rambunctious and full of vinegar. That was enough to make him stand out in any crowd, but there was something else that riveted my eyes, then repulsed them. I had to look away. It was obvious that he had been burned over much of his body. The sight was just too much for my senses. I tried to casually look into the eyes of the other children but my eyes became misty as my mind reeled. Horror, shock and wonder filled my mind.

The muffled sounds of people talking reminded me I was a guest there and needed to pay attention. I swallowed hard as a flash of unconscious embarrassment wafted over me. We put the trash bags in a closet and moved into a room with several picnic tables built a little close to the ground. The chaplain said a prayer, then we all stood in line as two women scooped food onto our plates. I don't exactly remember what we had to eat. I was overwhelmed with the experience after many days in the desert with little to do or see.

As I grabbed my cup and turned around to find a seat, I was torn by the scene before me. One of the orphanage staff was motioning me over to an adult table while some kids at a smaller table motioned me over to theirs. I knew the adult table would offer safe, interesting, polite conversation. But I was tired of playing it safe. I couldn't resist those little faces.

As I sat at the child's' table I felt like Gulliver sitting down with the Lilliputians. I had to cross my legs under the table like a pretzel in order to fit. The enthusiasm of the children drew me into their world. They were starved for attention; I was starved for recognition. They asked me simple questions like "where do you live" and "how old are you"? I started playing with my food to get them to laugh. I deliberately left some food on my face to get their attention.

"Hey, you've got food on your face", one of the little girls exclaimed! "I do", I said, as I acted surprised? I wiped it off and stuck a carrot in my ear. The children laughed. They knew I was trying to be funny for them at my expense. It was fun until an older boy at the next table started throwing food at our table. I made my exit at that point and moved over to the adult table. I let the orphanage personnel handle the situation…and the cleanup.

Everyone was encouraged to go back into the main room once the meal was finished. We handed the toys to the children and suddenly we were no longer the center of attention. I asked one of the orphanage workers about the story behind the boy who had been burned. She said that his family had been using a gasoline stove for cooking when it exploded, killing all of his family and leaving him with burns over eighty percent of his body. Infection was their biggest concern at this point. His immunity was very low. Later, he would have to undergo skin grafts and have the dead skin removed.

I had read about these things in a book about a soldier who had been burned in Vietnam. I remembered the excruciating pain and isolation the man had been through. It was too much to fathom how such a young boy could handle loosing his family and endure the upcoming medical procedures. She told me that every-one felt sorry for him and found it hard to discipline him. He had been asked if he wanted to see himself one day recently. The orphanage staff wanted to prepare him for the future. Mirrors had been hidden until they thought he was ready. He excitedly agreed. As they held the mirror in front of his face he looked at himself for just a second then turned away. He adamantly denied that the fellow in the mirror was he and said someone was playing tricks on him. Then he scurried off to play with the other children.

The Chaplain said it was time to go. Most of the kids kept playing with their toys as we waved goodbye. However, the little girl I had sat across at lunch came over clutching a doll. She looked up at me with large round eyes and suddenly grabbed my leg. One of the orphanage staff walked over and tugged at her gently to let me go. She looked at me again and asked if I would be back. I crouched down, looked her eye to eye, and told her I didn't know. I wanted to give her a hug. Instead the little girl scrunched her tiny face in disgust and ran away to the other side of the room.

I felt hurt that I couldn't tell her I would be back. But I knew this trip was a fluke. I had no transportation and no permission to come back. The last thing these kids needed was someone telling them they would be there for them and then never showing again. As we left the orphanage I was glad that I had made the trip. I hoped that my being there had helped the kids in some way. I knew they had helped me. For the first time in months I had heard the laughter of children and temporarily thrown off the responsibility of being a Staff Sergeant in the Cavalry.

I felt more human, more alive, and more thankful. I wondered what kind of future these kids had in front of them. In ten years where would they be? Would the boy with the burns survive his injuries? It was overwhelming when I thought of the possibilities. I was glad that at least these children had someone to look after them and care for them at the present time.

God only knew what lay in store for these children of turmoil. I prayed that whatever lay in store for them that their lives from here forward would be much better than what had happened in the past. I will never forget these orphaned children of Kuwait.

25

Our First Shower And The Missing .45

We couldn't believe it. We were going to get a shower after weeks without one. Sure, we had been cleaning ourselves with a washcloth and an ammo can full of water, but it just wasn't the same. Having someone pour a can full of water over your head so the shampoo would be rinsed is different than standing under a flow of water from a shower. I remembered our showers at the apartments in Al Kobar towers. The water wasn't very hot but it was so much better than cleaning yourself out of an ammo can.

Looking back on it now it seemed to be a heady experience. There was privacy, hot water and when you were done you felt clean. When cleaning yourself with only a washcloth you were restricted to how much water you could use. After you were finished, no matter how hard you tried, looking back into a dirty can of water you never felt truly clean. We all wanted to feel clean again. We wanted to feel the steam of a shower again and not have to look at dirty water when we were through.

We gathered our shower gear and I put mine in a wet weather bag. These were bags made out of rubber with a tie string at the top to keep water away from your clothes. These kept our clothes and equipment in our duffel bags dry and dust-free no matter what the weather. I put a change of clothes with green wool socks, brown cotton underwear and t-shirt inside. To this I added my shaving kit, a large green towel and washcloth, and a pair of waterproof slippers.

We were told that we had to stay in full combat uniform including carrying our weapons. I added my boot polishing kit and put the bag at the end of the Bradleys' ramp. I noticed that several of us were taking a wet weather bag so I pulled out my pen and wrote my last name in block letters on the side of my bag. With this many men taking showers it would be easy to get the wrong gear.

The truck arrived and we all climbed inside. We were giddy with excitement. We relished the thought of hot steamy showers and being able to lather ourselves as much as we wanted. Someone said they would take two showers just to get totally clean. Another said he would have so much lather on his body that no one would recognize him. "Just don't drop your soap" another quipped. We all laughed. It was a reminder that we were all sexually deprived and it was a release of tension to joke that someone might be so horny as to take advantage of the situation if he saw someone bent over in the shower. We all trusted each other. My whole career I never heard of anyone taking advantage of someone in this way. In a shower naked with a bunch of other guys you are at your most vulnerable. Rank and privilege have no place in a shower. At these times camaraderie and trust are all that separate a man from hell.

After about half an hour we arrived at the shower point. As we jumped down from the truck an NCO from the shower point greeted us. On a board near the entrance to the showers were the posted rules. As he went over these rules I looked around. The shower point consisted of two medium size army tents with a truck mounting a portable generator parked nearby. Past the truck was a huge black rubber water bladder with a hose running to a pump and a hose running from the pump to the tent.

Rule number one: anyone not following instructions would be asked to leave. Rule two: no horseplay; no towel snapping, no water fights. Rule three: follow the instructions of the shower personnel. Our instructor told us to ground our combat gear on the ground outside the first tent. Half the group would shower while the other half watched the combat gear and vice versa. The LBE (load bearing equipment) was to be formed into a circle with the protective mask inside the circle, our helmet on top, and our weapon on the right side.

We were then to enter the first tent, take our clothes off and enter the second tent. Once inside we were to find a showerhead and stand under it. We would receive a one-minute release of water then the water would be shut off. During this time we were to lather and wait for the second release of water. This would last about two minutes. Then we would dry off back in the first tent and put on clean clothes. We had ten minutes to finish and get back to our gear so that the next group could enter the tent. "Any questions" he asked?

"Yeah" someone said, "where are all the girls"? We all laughed. What a concept! This guy sure had some imagination. What chaotic situation that would be, however wonderful it might seem at first. "The women's showers are about five miles south of here," he said. "And they're guarded" he added with a smile. We all chuckled at his remarks and headed for the area outside the tent where we were to ground our gear. "The first ten men ready file into the tent", ordered the NCO.

Immediately there was a mad dash for the tent. Unfortunately I was a distance from the tent and not quite ready to go in. I would have to wait for the next group. Those of us who had not been the first ten inside got our gear out of our bags and sat around talking. Sergeant Beets had not made it inside either. He walked over to me and sat down. In only a few minutes there was a call for the next ten men. We gathered our things and went into the first tent.

Inside were benches on either side with piles of the first groups' gear stacked everywhere. I found a small empty space on a bench and put my gear underneath. As we stripped down to our birthday suits I felt a little self-conscious as I always did when I was naked in front of my peers. All of us smelled a little ripe. Because we knew we were getting a shower none of us had washed before we got on the truck. Armpit odor and crotch rot mingled with foot odor and bad breath. Someone laughed that they could see dingle berries on someone's butt. A guy flushed with embarrassment quickly wrapped a towel around his waist and remarked that at least he didn't have a brown stripe in his underwear. We all laughed.

We could here remarks from the first group as we undressed. It was clear there would be no hot water. Even though the sun had warmed the water in the large water bladders it would not be as warm as it had at Al Kobar towers. Comments from those exiting the showers ran from gratefulness to be clean again to how cold the water felt. I began to wonder about the temperature of the water and prepared myself for the shock. I had my towel wrapped around my waist the same as most others, both hands full of soap, shampoo, conditioner and washcloth.

As we entered the second tent each of us had to step up onto wooden palettes placed on the sand to allow for water runoff. Bare light bulbs had been strung in the top of the tent to provide light. The light bulbs cast shadows on the walls of the tent and accentuated skin that had not been darkened by sunlight. "Look at that farmers tan" someone pointed out. We all laughed again. Almost all of us were in the same condition. Our arms, faces and necks were darkly tanned from exposure to the sun. The rest of our bodies were as pink as a newborn babies skin.

I tried to find a place to put my towel, but there weren't any hooks. I draped it over the showerhead and put the shampoo and conditioner next to the palettes, keeping the soap in my hand. "You have one minute. Here comes the water," said a booming voice. A generator began to hum and the pipes above us gave a shudder. Suddenly the showerheads closest to the water pump sprang to life as each shower in succession sprayed a fine mist over our bodies. Gasps and expletives cut the air as the cold water hit our naked bodies. Shudders hit us as we each tried to lessen the effects of the cold.

My skin crawled over my back and up my neck until it reached the top of my head. Then it rushed down my forehead and almost made my eyes pop. My mouth fell wide open and froze in a strange expression similar to the painting *The Scream*. Others were reacting similarly. Some seemed to actually enjoy the effect and verbally jabbed at those of us who didn't, questioning our manhood. Slowly the water temperature and our body temperature approached continuity and we actually began to enjoy the experience as we quickly lathered our bodies.

The water stopped and it was comical to see so many naked men partially lathered with soap. We all continued to lather. At some point all of us had done as much as we could. Standing there with soap in our eyes, fighting to see our surroundings, we felt stupid. "They must be out of water", someone said. A nervous chuckle went through the group. "Hey, turn the water on", some yelled. "We are on break" came the reply from outside the tent. Groans of agony and roars of irritation erupted from all of us. How ridiculous was the scene. How hurt were these shower personnel going to be if they didn't turn the water back on immediately! "Just joking", came a calm voice as the water sprayed from our showerheads. "I'm gonna kill that guy", one said. "You'll have to get in line behind me", said another. "Bastard", swore another.
We finished showering and the water was cut off just as we were relishing the experience. The heat from our bodies rose in an eerie mist to the ceiling of the tent.

I shuddered as my skin reacted to the warmth of the first tent. I quickly dried my skin and hair with the towel as I searched for my bag. There it was under the bench where I left it. Sitting above it was a man pulling on his socks. It looked like he could be there a while so I asked him to move over so I could get my bag. He seemed embarrassed and quickly moved over several inches, grabbing his gear as he went.

Sitting on the bench I tried hard not to look at anyone else. There was no dignity here. It had all vanished when we first walked through the tent flap. "Sorry", came a voice from the other side of the tent. "Oh man", said a coughing, sputtering voice near him. "Damn it", yelled another! "You SOB", screamed another. "I said I was sorry. It just slipped out", said the first voice. "Man, you'd better not break wind in the truck or I'm tossing you out", threatened another as he quickly walked out the door of the tent. I held my breath as I finished dressing, snorting small amounts of air near the tent wall when needed. "How disgusting", I thought. Some men no matter how talented or courageous were just baboons at heart.

As I surveyed the floor of our tent I wondered if I would catch something. Bits of toilet paper, dirty underwear and spit were everywhere except on the path to the door. Even though it was good to feel clean all over, the experience had been less than wonderful. I walked outside and found my gear. It was all there. Sergeant Beets was still in the tent. I drank some water and polished my boots while I waited. Since everything else was clean my boots stood out. The boots absorbed the polish like a sponge absorbs water. I gave them a second coat.

Sergeant Beets came out swinging his waterproof bag and smiling. "What do you think", I queried? "That was great", he exclaimed! I wondered what had happened to give him that impression. The truck arrived and we climbed in under the canvass. The trip back was hot because little air was moving inside. We all broke sweat. To increase our discomfort every time the truck slowed down the talcum powder desert dust rushed between every crack where the canvas was not tightly sealed. It especially rolled in through the back flap where it was not tied to the truck. By the time we arrived at our assembly area we were all covered with dust and sweating beneath our clothes. I decided that a shower under these circumstances was just not worth it.

The next time a truck pulled in to take us to the showers I declined to go and decided to use the privacy accorded by their absence. I filled an ammo can with water and laid my poncho on the ground. After stripping naked behind my Bradley I took the water and, standing on the poncho, I poured half of it over myself. I lathered my hair and body, then fumbled for the remainder of the water.

Once all the water was poured I realized that I still had shampoo in my hair. I looked around to see if there was anyone that had noticed I was naked. Everyone was gone except for one person manning the radio and a few others napping. I felt a sense of freedom not having to reveal my nakedness to others, but still stand naked in the desert. That feeling flashed away as I saw someone stirring across the assembly area. I realized I had better finish and dried everything except my hair. I dressed in clean clothes from the waist down, filled the ammo can half full of water from our tan plastic five-gallon water cans and rinsed my hair thoroughly. Then I climbed to the top of my Bradley and let the sun tan my chest and back. This was so much better than the shower experience. I could even have a little privacy.

When Sergeant Beets returned from his shower the first thing he said was that his pistol was missing. When he finished his shower he did a thorough inspection of the area but couldn't find his gear. I told him I would have to tell Sergeant Z and find out what he wanted us to do. Sergeant Z told us to go back to the showers and look for the weapon again. The rest of the gear could be replaced, but not the weapon. We were to call him with the results. If we hadn't found it by then he would have to tell the Lieutenant.

We got in our Bradley and headed to the showers. When we arrived at the showers we dismounted and walked the area where soldiers' gear was grounded. Several soldiers were already putting on their gear. Sergeant Beets checked any that looked like it might be his. Soldiers who were there told him which ones were unclaimed. Out of these only one had a pistol. I pointed at the pistol and asked Sergeant Beets if it was his. He made reference to the holster. He said his had green tape on it, this one didn't. I should have made him verify the serial number of the weapon.

I knew that green tape could be removed or fall off once the adhesive dried out in the desert heat. But I didn't want to embarrass him by forcing the issue. I'll never know if that was indeed his weapon. I radioed Sergeant Z that we had not found the weapon. He informed the lieutenant. The company commander was informed and every soldier in the company was made to verify their serial numbers. At the same time queries were made of everyone, including the shower staff, as to any items that had been found. Sergeant Beets was on the promotion board roster. The command was wondering whether to keep his name on the list.

The next morning someone from the shower staff turned in the pistol as well as the rest of his gear. Sergeant Beets was made to get it from the Company Commander. He had to explain himself and restore the confidence of the command in his leadership. He impressed the leadership and his name was kept on the promotion roster. Shortly thereafter he passed the board needed to progress to the next rank, given by a board consisting of the Command Sergeant Major as board chairman and the First Sergeant from each company in the battalion filling the rest of the board. I was very proud of Sergeant Beets and knew he would make a fine Staff Sergeant. I will always consider him my friend as well.

26

The Phone Call Home

The war was over and now everyone wanted to call home. But how do you find a phone in the desert? You have the Department of Defense contract a portable phone center with a satellite link, that's how. Yes, Lt. Wynn told us, a phone center had been set up where we could call home. We were excited! We thought we would have to reach Saudi Arabia before we would be able to make a phone call. Best of all, the phone call would be free! And we could make as many phone calls as we wanted.

We all thought this was too good to be true. Had the Saudis given us a lot of money to be able to do this? Had the American people donated this because we were heroes? We really didn't care. We just wanted to call home and here a familiar voice. We wanted to tell everyone that we were OK in this awful desert.

The day finally arrived when we were scheduled to go to the phone center. Rumors had trickled back from other platoons that had gone to place phone calls that not all was as we had been led to believe. Initially we had wondered why it would be days before we would be able to make a phone call. I figured it probably had to do with a shortage of vehicles to take us to the phone center. Now we were hearing stories of long lines before you actually got to the phone center. We also heard that there was a limit on the amount of time we could spend on the phone. Then there was the story that indeed you could make as many phone calls as you wanted, but after your first phone call you had to go to the back of the line and wait until it was your turn again before you could make another.

We all were disheartened by these stories, but we were accustomed to waiting in lines. We boarded the two-and-a-half ton truck and headed east. The truck wound its way over narrow dusty trails until we saw huge power lines overhead with an asphalt road running beside them. We followed this road for a while until a stench as foul as anything I have ever smelled overcame us. We all coughed, gagged and covered our mouths for a few seconds. Away from the road only a few hundred feet lay a flock of dead sheep, looking as if they had died in an instant, many of them charred black on one side. Some of the grass around them had burnt as well.

The heat of the day accentuated the pungent aroma. Only a few hundred feet further and we were at the entrance to the phone center, located next to a huge building, similar to an aircraft hanger, with a large hole in it. As we got off the truck we could see a yellow hamburger stand with a red roof. I checked my watch to see what time it would be stateside where my parents lived and realized they would still be in bed. Besides, it was close to lunchtime and the line at the hamburger stand was only three or four deep. I decided to get a burger before getting in line. As I approached the Hamburger stand I could tell from the aroma that this was not going to be like McDonalds. The hamburgers were free and as most things in life, you get what you pay for. It tasted almost exactly like the one I had had at the Air Force Base in Riyadh. I tried to make it taste better by adding some condiments but there was little left. There were no pickles, onions, or lettuce.

Only packets of mustard, ketchup and relish remained. I resigned myself to the modest little burger, a bottle of water and a small bag of generic potato chips. I had only taken a couple of bites of my burger and some chips when the wind changed direction. Suddenly the wind, which had been blowing the stench of the rotting sheep away from my location, shifted to blowing directly at me. My gag reflex immediately kicked in and sent part of the burger in my mouth back onto the plate from whence it came.

My eyes welled with tears as they instinctively closed shut against the onslaught. I gagged trying to take a small breath of air as my whole body reeled from the effect. Thankfully the wind shifted again just as quickly and I could take a long breath of semi-clean air. I decided that it was pointless to proceed with eating anything and queried at the IQ of the person responsible for putting this hamburger stand at this location. It made sense now why the line had been so short at the hamburger stand.

As I proceeded to the area marked out for phone calls I was surprised that I couldn't see anything. The whole phone center setup had been placed inside a ring of high sand dunes for protection from the wind. Climbing over the sand dune on a small path I stopped to view the scene to see where I needed to go next. My mouth dropped open. I could not believe my eyes. Before me were several large military tents with a line of soldiers in front of each of them. Each line of soldiers numbered 20 to 30. As someone prompted me from behind to move forward I comforted myself with the thought that my parents would most certainly be awake when I called them.

While waiting in line I tried to find something to occupy my time. I searched the long lines to see if I recognized anyone I had served with from previous tours of duty. I read the large signs in front of each tent, which stated the rules for making a phone call. Rule 1: One phone call at a time. You must go to the end of the line to make another call. Rule 2: No call will be over 5 minutes. At the end of 5 minutes the phone will automatically be disconnected. Rule 3: You must sign in, giving the phone numbers of your first and second choices. When the operator has reached your party, you will be called into the tent in the order of the sign-in roster.

There were other rules, too about keeping the tents clean, etc., but these were the important ones. I began to formulate what I was going to say in five minutes. So much had happened since I had last talked with my parents. I felt a pang in my heart as I heard other soldiers talking with their wives and girlfriends. A small tear welled up in the corner of my eye as I realized that I had no one waiting for me in Germany. I cleared the lump out of my throat, wiped the tear from my eye nonchalantly so as not to raise any suspicion and straitened my uniform. I was determined not to feel sorry for myself, so I just put those thoughts out of my mind.

Out of the crowd someone said, "Hey Sergeant Abbott!" I turned to see one of the men I had enlisted in the Army when I was a recruiter. It was David Weekley. We shook hands as I asked him how he had been. He said he had been good. He was assigned as a mechanic in my division. It was good to see him and touch bases with him. As an Army Recruiter I always wondered what had happened to the soldiers I had a part in enlisting. (After I got back to Germany I read the names of the soldiers who had died to see if any of them had been ones I had recruited. None were.)

"Abbott, you're next," said the woman at the door to the tent. "Phone number six. Just pick up the receiver and listen for the operator." I went to a folding table and sat at the phone labeled six. As I quickly picked up the phone I tried to remember what I was going to tell my parents. My palms began to sweat and my mouth went dry. "Your party is on the line, please hold" came the directions over the phone. "Yello" came my mothers' distinctive voice over the phone. Immediately I felt relaxed. The words and thoughts I had decided to use disappeared.

I didn't know what to say except that I was well. I told her that I only had 5 minutes to talk. She seemed confused by this so I told her about the phone center set up in the desert via satellite and the long lines to make a phone call. I had waited over an hour and a half to talk to my parents. Mom told Dad to get on the other line so they could both talk. While he was walking to the other extension, Mom told me that he had been watching CNN till late in the night and going to church, something he hadn't done in years.

Dad answered the phone in the usual way, making it seem as if I was just down the block rather than 7,000 miles away. He asked what the weather was like as he always did. I tried to impress him with the fact that we were talking via a satellite link from a remote location in the desert. He said uh-huh and changed the subject to my health. I repeated that I was fine and had actually had a shower a few days earlier. He didn't seem to grasp the concept that this was a rare, wonderful luxury for soldiers like me.

The time on my watch said the five minutes were almost over so I told them so and began to say my good-byes. Mom seemed to ignore what I had said and began telling me about some other news as the line went suddenly dead. I sat for a second to gather my thoughts then walked slowly out of the tent. The desert seemed even larger now. The sky seemed to stretch forever. The seven thousand miles now seemed like seven million. The truck was due back in 45 minutes. There was nothing left to do but wait for the returning truck.

27

Shop Like An Arabian

The rumors were true. We were going to visit Kuwait City! A few soldiers didn't want to go. What was there to see, a destroyed city? What was there to buy? If they didn't have a McDonalds, why go? But this was not my attitude. I wanted to experience what it was like to walk through an Arab city. The visit to the air base in Riyadh was nice and the visit to the Christian mission in Kuwait City was a unique experience, but I just hadn't experienced the flavor of the Middle East. Both times Americans had surrounded me. We had been told that on this trip we would get to go downtown to shop and go to the top of the space needle that overlooked the Persian Gulf. I was excited to be able to go on this trip. As an added bonus we would be able to shed all our combat gear and wear just our uniform, boots and "soft cap" (BDU cap).

The deuce and a half arrived and we climbed into the back. It was so nice to be getting out of the assembly area again. The truck took us over to the company assembly area to store our weapons, buy Kuwaiti dinars and get a briefing from the XO (Executive Officer). We stood in line and handed in our weapons to the armorer. Inside his tent were rows of heavy metal racks. The racks were chained together with heavy chain and each rack was individually locked.

The XO then got us in a circle and briefed us on what we could and couldn't do in Kuwait City. We would be allowed to visit only the open-air market in the center of the city for one hour. Then we would be loaded back onto the truck and taken to the space needle. We were reminded to show proper respect for the Kuwaiti's and that if we got in trouble the Kuwaitis would have jurisdiction. Once they were finished with us, which might include slicing off our hand for theft, then the Army would impose its sentence. I looked at my hand and reminded myself to do nothing that would even possibly be taken as such. We were directed to a lieutenant sitting behind a portable desk with a cash box.

We would be able to get a cash advance on our pay that could be taken in dollars or dinars or a combination of both. I decided to take the advance and get part of it in dinars. The Kuwaitis could do a currency exchange if I found something I really liked but didn't have enough dinars to purchase. However, Kuwaiti dinars could not be exchanged back into dollars. I didn't want to get stuck with a fistful of dinars I couldn't use.

We climbed back in the truck and waited for the others to get their money. It seemed like an eternity. I wanted to shout, "just get on the truck and move out. There aren't any women or alcohol for sale so most of you won't need any money". I knew it to be true. In peacetime most of these soldiers just wanted to get drunk and find a woman to have sex. Even though Kuwaitis were more liberal that their Arab neighbors, neither one of these things could be found here. I doubted many of them would appreciate this trip like I would. I was concerned that since these soldiers had been in the desert for months, a sudden burst of freedom could spell disaster. I would have to keep an eye on them while I tried to appreciate the city and its people.

The ride into the city was bumpy and dusty. Even with the flap closed on the back of the truck the fine talcum-like powder of the desert rolled in through the cracks every time the truck slowed. We finally hit pavement and we all breathed deeply as the faster speed and lack of dust blew fresh air inside the canvas-covered truck. Two soldiers near the tailgate flipped the flap up so that we could all see out. For a while all we could see was desert. Then on either side of the road we passed hundreds of burned and bombed Iraqi military and civilian vehicles. There were huge buses, trucks, cars, vans, APC's, antiaircraft vehicles and tanks.

This was the highway of death we had heard about. There were some vehicles that were very close to the edge of the road. As we passed them we could see numerous flies and smell the stench of death. Even though the dead bodies had been removed, the aftereffects were still telling. Again I was thankful the air force had taken care of this threat. Air power had been so decisive in this war. I felt sympathetic for these Iraqi soldiers for just a second. Then I remembered what these same soldiers had done to the people of Kuwait. I quickly concluded that they deserved what they got.

As we came into the city someone at the front of the truck said they could see an amusement park. OK, who was pulling my leg? I thought. Others thought the same thing. We turned a corner and there it was, a huge amusement park with a large parking lot. The park was full of trees and looked totally out of place in the desert.

I could see a Ferris wheel, a roller coaster, and several other rides. Someone asked if we could stop. The officer in charge said no, that when the Iraqis left Kuwait they booby-trapped the amusement part. The Kuwaitis were considering whether to try and disarm the booby traps or just to level the park. Experts in explosives had given the assessment that it would be so risky to disarm the booby traps, that to do it correctly could take as long as two years.

The nearer we got to the city center, the more traffic we encountered. The one thing that struck me was the fact that almost every driver, who were all men, drove with only one hand. The other hand would be holding a set of beads similar to those Catholics use to pray the rosary. I was told later they were Muslim prayer beads. The drivers would be thumbing these beads while they drove, praying that they wouldn't have a wreck. It seemed to me that if they put the beads down and put the other hand on the wheel, they might not have to pray so hard.

The driver parked the truck and we all jumped down. The XO had us gather around him. He told us the truck would remain in this spot and that we had one hour to visit the shops. He gave us the boundaries of the area we were to stay in and said if we were late the truck would leave without us. An Article 15 (non judicial punishment) would be waiting on us when the MP's brought us back to the AA.

Soldiers divided into small groups or walked singly down the narrow streets. I wanted to stay by myself to look at things at a distance, then home in on things that interested me. Initially I wanted to just observe the life of this older part of the city to see how it compared with life in the United States or Germany. I knew that if I were with others, they would distract me.

The first thing I noticed was that the streets were not level. After being in the broad, flat desert for months it was very noticeable. It wasn't drastic; it wasn't planned. And the streets were not straight, either. The whole area just seemed to meander, kind of like some old towns I had discovered in Germany. But this was different. Everyone except we soldiers were dressed in Arab dress, just like a scene out of Ali Babba or Arabian Nights. And the faces. Almost everyone's' face was dark, not only because they were Arab, but because of living out in the intense sunlight.

Some of the older men had darker faces, worn and wrinkled by the sun, with sunken eyes full of anguish. I wondered what they had seen in life that made their faces seem like they were in such pain. But as I and my fellow soldiers approached, these faces brightened at the corners and an expression of calm and happiness washed over them. But their eyes never changed. These merchants didn't pressure us to buy anything as I thought they would. They just invited us into their shops and, if they spoke English, described what they had for sale. If they didn't speak English, as was usually the case, they would just point to different items and nod their heads agreeably or gesticulate in a way that attempted to make us understand what they sold.

I expected to see locally made garments, shoes, toys, etc. What I found was that all of their garments as well as their shoes were made in other places like Korea, or the Philippines. Most of the toys were from the United States or Europe. But then I began to smell some wonderful aromas. I didn't recognize anything I smelled, but I knew these smells were not from Europe or the United States. A couple of guys from my platoon walked up from a side street and wanted to walk with me. Just then an Arab man standing in front of a small storefront behind a small table motioned to us to come over.

On the table were huge clumps of some kind of fruit or vegetable. I didn't know what they were, but they had been prepared in many different ways. Some were dried. Others had been candied and dipped in sugar, sesame seeds and other things. There didn't seem to be a smell to them. My companions and I were offered some of these by the vendor and the two of them began to eat them. I wanted to know what they were. The vendor got a strained look on his face, stared across the street for a second, then said in a thick accent "figs". I had never had a fig, except in Fig Newton's, and felt compelled to try them. I knew this was food which hadn't been cooked, but when would I ever get another chance like this?

I took one of the candied ones with sesame seeds stuck to it and bit the end off. It was delicious! I ate the rest of it and relished the experience. But now I had sticky fingers and no way to clean them. I declined to buy any, wondering how long such food would keep. I could only eat a little at a time since they were so rich. I knew I wouldn't finish them before they went bad.

I looked around for a bathroom to wash my hands, but I had no idea what the sign for a men's bathroom looked like. The last thing I wanted was to walk into some place I wasn't supposed to be. I crudely licked the stickiness off my fingers and found a fountain to wash my hands. My fingers weren't clean, but at least they were cleaner.

As I looked up from the fountain I saw an old heavyset woman in a complete black burka with a mesh face piece. She was sitting on the street with her legs crossed. She was begging for us to give her whatever we could spare. Across the street I saw another one, then down a side street another one. Other soldiers were giving the beggars a few dinars. I had no idea how much I was going to spend, but I made a note to myself to give them whatever I had left when I was finished. As I walked by her I could smell that she hadn't washed in a few days. The whole scene made me think back to scenes out of the Bible. I couldn't believe that such things were going on in the twentieth century. Then I remembered that we had our own homeless people.

The closer I got to the center of the market the more pungent the aromas became. There was the aroma of saffron, sage, ginger, thyme and cloves as well as many others. As I walked along my sense of smell was wonderfully stimulated by the experience. It was just as I had dreamed when I read of the Middle East as a young boy. I nearly expected to see a young boy with a flying carpet. On a side street near the corner of a small square I saw a young woman sitting in front of a rug displaying jewelry. She wore a black robe with a black lacy scarf over her hair. She was pretty in a simple, classic way.

I walked over to take a look at her display. As I approached she didn't stand up so I crouched down to take a closer look and be on her level. I looked up and could tell she looked a little nervous, her mouth taut, her eyes darting to the side then darting back to me. It was then that I noticed a young Arab man in white walking toward us from the left.

He was nice and relaxed on the surface, but had an inner toughness that made me realize I had just made a faux pas. I had forgotten that I wasn't supposed to talk to an Arab woman without her husband or a male relative being present. The man answered my questions in broken English and I politely moved on. As I walked away I looked to see if the man would make a scene with the woman. He didn't. He just slowly walked away.

I purchased a bowl of hot, steaming soup from one of the vendors. It was so good that I held each spoonful in my mouth for a second before I swallowed the wonderful mixture. Maybe it was the fact that I had been living on Army food for the last few months that made my palette and nostrils feel like I was in heaven. I don't know. All I know is that that bowl of soup was one of the best I've ever had.

I looked at my watch; it was time to move back to where the truck was parked. I didn't want to go. I wanted to stay and get to know these people better. Just then I remembered my thought to give the women beggars what remained of my dinars. As I retraced my steps I looked at the spots where I had seen the beggars. They were gone. I felt upset. I had no idea where they had gone. As I walked toward the truck I fell into a group of soldiers telling each other about what they had seen. Many of them had appreciated the same things I had seen and heard and none of them had gotten into trouble. I was so proud of them. Could these be the same men who were fighting each other before the war?

We crawled into the truck and rode over to the space needle. The space needle in Kuwait looks similar to a giant golf ball with a large toothpick stuck through the middle. It dominates the skyline and can be seen for quite a distance. It sits on the East Side of Kuwait City near the gulf. After the truck parked in the parking lot we jumped out of the back and were astounded at the sight.

Towering over us was the huge space needle. I felt like an ant on a golf green waiting for someone to tee off. As we walked inside the entrance I was surprised to not see a security guard or doorman. There were nice glass enclosures which at one time had merchants, but which were now empty. The floors and walls seemed a little bland but were made of a nice light pink marble. We made our way over to the elevator and punched the up button. It seemed like forever while we waited for the elevator to come down. We wondered how tall this structure was and speculated on what we would see at the top.

The officer in charge said that there was a restaurant at the top but it wasn't open for business just yet. It would be a few weeks before they could find staff and the food began to arrive. The elevator couldn't hold us all so half of us had to wait until the elevator returned again. I used this time to walk around inside the lobby. I could see the water of the Arabian Sea lapping against the shore and some tropical plants that had been planted around the base of the tower. It was nice to see so much water after months in the desert. It refreshed my soul and nourished my outlook on life.

Yes, at some point we would leave this desert and see the real world again. It gave me palatable hope. Noisy activity near the elevator alerted me to the elevators' arrival. My group now packed into the medium-sized elevator. When was the last time I had been in an elevator? I couldn't remember. We didn't have any in my hometown. There weren't any for over one hundred miles in any direction. It must have been when I was in St. Louis that I last rode an elevator. That building was over thirty stories tall and the office I was visiting was near the top.

As I was invited into the office I could see that the entire outside wall was made of polarized glass. The view was spectacular. I could see over half of the city and the edge of the airport. But as I approached the glass my vertigo began to make my knees wobble and my head spin. I stepped away from the huge glass window.

The ding-ding sound and the effects of the elevator slowing down shook me out of my daydream and made me realize we were at the top. Since this was an express elevator I was surprised that it had taken so long to get to the top. The doors opened and we were almost blinded by the light. Sunlight was pouring in huge glass windows from floor to ceiling. To my right was a cola machine, unplugged and empty. A cold soda would certainly hit the spot. My group quickly made its way to the windows for a better look.

As I walked toward the windows I could feel the structure move ever so slightly. I lost my balance for a split second so I stopped to recover. I decided moving to the window was not such a good idea. I moved close enough to be able to see the distant sights from the tower. Looking straight down from that height just didn't have any appeal for me. One of the guys urged me to go to the window and look down to experience the effects of our elevation. I politely declined.

I saw a bathroom out of the corner of my eye and told him necessity called as I walked toward it. I was glad that at least this building had international symbols on their bathrooms. The marble floor continued into the bathroom and carried up the walls. The bathroom looked like any I had seen in the United States, seeming modest for the building. At last my hands were clean! I walked back into the open area and proceeded to look from all four points of the compass. The view was breathtaking.

To the east I could see the vastness of the Arabian Sea to a sliver of land on the horizon. Wow; I could see Iran! To the north my eye traced the coastline from the port of Kuwait to the horizon. I was sure that at the farthest point had to be Iraq. Just to my left I could see a few oil fires in the distance. I looked to the west and saw almost the whole city and far into the desert. I strained to see the location of our assembly area. I saw a few indistinct shapes but couldn't identify anything. I guess our camouflage worked well.

To the left I could see many oil wells still burning, their thick black smoke billowing to the west in plumes that seemed to reach heaven. To the right I saw what appeared to be thousands of black ants near the main highway heading north out of Kuwait City. It was the highway of death. From this vantage point I could see the extent of the damage much better. It seemed to go on for miles. I had to look away. If things hadn't gone as well as they did during the war, that could've been us. I could make out the amusement park after my eye was drawn to the Ferris wheel. It seemed so small compared to those of the United States.

To the south my eye followed the coastline. I could see the waves lapping against the shore. I wished we could go to the beach and wade in the water. I could just make out the city of Khafji. It seemed so close when viewed from up there. In the distant haze of the gulf I could make out the outline of a supertanker loaded with oil headed to ports unknown. I figured it must be from Iran, possibly from Iraq, but definitely not from Kuwait. It was highly unlikely that Kuwait was in a position to pump oil to the port and load a supertanker. I thought that I would be able to see some of our ships, maybe an aircraft carrier battle group. Only the giant tanker could be seen on that vast body of water.

It was time to go. The first group reluctantly shuffled into the waiting elevator as I gathered my thoughts. I had come through a war to be able to see this place. I was glad that someone had thought it right for us to be able to see the country we had helped to liberate. This experience would give us something to talk and write home about. There is only so much you can say about living in the desert.

Now we were headed back to the desert to the same routine. I had stopped thinking about when we would go back to Germany, let alone home to see friends and family. It was just too depressing to contemplate.

28

Was It True?

It was true. We were finally getting Desert Camouflage BDU's. After almost five months in the desert, three months *after* the war ended and almost every soldier had deployed back to Germany or the states, we were getting issued new uniforms. I tried to control my enthusiasm as I walked back from the platoon meeting but a smile kept breaking across my face. This was the first good news we had heard since we were told of the trip to Kuwait City. But this news was different. This news meant for sure that we were going home soon.

Sergeant Z had told us that the reason we were getting these uniforms was for the return trip to Germany. The leadership wanted us to look like desert warriors, not soldiers who looked like they had spent the war on the sidelines. "I want your shirt, pant, hat and boot sizes on a piece of paper right now", I told my men. "Why do you want that", Allen said, "don't you already have it in your little book"?

"Yes", I said, "I've got it in my little book. But some of you have changed a little since we started. Some of you have lost weight, some have gained muscle, and some of your heads have swelled a little", I said with a chuckle. This last item was a reference to the things some would say about their actions after they arrived home. Some in the platoon had bragged how they would tell huge exaggerations about what we did, hoping to gain more glory from their friends and family. "I need these sizes so supply can send us Desert Camouflage BDU's in the correct sizes", I said. "Why would we need Desert BDU's now", Burns said?

"We need them for the plane trip home", I said, a huge smile breaking across my face. Shouts of joy rang out across the star as crews got the word. Soldiers began high-fiving each other, running over to their friends on other crews to share the joy. "When are we leaving", Sergeant Beets asked, now alone on the

151

Bradley? "I still don't know", I said, "but it looks like in the next two to three weeks. They want us to start inventories on all the equipment and have it ready for turn-in". Sergeant Beets' smile grew larger. We could all see the end of the journey now.

The next day Sergeant Z told us that tomorrow supply would bring us the BDU's. Wow, I thought, that was fast. Supply doesn't usually work that fast. The next morning an Army truck arrived with several large square cardboard boxes. The mortars and scouts gathered around as we waited for our names to be called off and handed our uniforms. The truck driver headed out of the gate, throwing plumes of dust into the air as he went. Sergeant Z and the Sergeant Montgomery opened the boxes and looked at us.

"Everyone find your size and try them on. Each man only gets one set. Once the shortages are corrected we will be issued a second set", SFC Montgomery said. I felt panic as I saw soldiers begin pulling brand new Desert Camouflage BDU's out of the boxes, boxes that were already half empty. Someone handed me a pair of pants that were two sizes too small. A soldier on the other side of the box held aloft a pair of pants that were larger than any I had ever seen. "Looks like Taylor gets this pair", he said smiling. Taylor was a mortar soldier who stood well over six feet tall and loved to eat. "Hey, none of these pants are the right size", someone mused.

I suddenly felt greed like never before. I reached into the box and pulled out pair after pair of pants. He was right. The first five pair were either much too large or too small. I handed each pair back to those behind me as I frantically searched for a pair that fit. Reason had left me. The fear that I would be wearing a uniform that made me look like a clown permeated my being. Finally I found a pair that might fit. Another pair I had grabbed with the first pair had the same waist size, but the legs were longer. I quickly judged the length against my legs and decided to go with the pants with the longer legs. I handed the other pair to a soldier standing next to me. "Thanks, Sergeant Abbott, I think these will fit", he said.

My heart beat a little slower now. I felt bad that I had been so greedy trying to find myself a pair of good fitting pants. I walked over to the box with the shirts. I found one that looked like it might fit. There were no markings to indicate the size. I then walked over to the box of boots and sorted through the small stack.

There were none my size. There were no hats. It was clear to all of us that we were getting the leftovers from all the other units. Why had we even turned in the list with our sizes? This was madness.

I walked over to my Bradley and put the pants and shirt on the front slope. I took off my woodland BDU's and pulled on the desert BDU's. It felt good to get new clothes. The shirt fit well but was a little short. The pant legs felt tight and the length was a little long. I looked back over to the boxes that had been thoroughly picked through. I decided to keep the set. I made a list of items that were still needed for my section and submitted them to Sergeant Z. I wondered if we would ever get the rest of our gear. I pictured myself arriving in Germany with black boots and no hat in ill-fitting BDU's. At least the pants wouldn't look like they belonged to MC Hammer.

We weren't allowed to wear the Desert BDU's until all of us had at least one full issue. We reluctantly pulled the woodland BDU's back on and packed the items we had just received inside our bags. When would we get the rest of our gear? No one knew. Two days later a supply truck arrived at our assembly area unannounced. Three more boxes were dropped off. This time there was little panic. Again there were no lists.

I found one pair of boots and a shirt that fit. I still needed another pair of boots and a pair of pants. Again, there were no hats. We were now allowed to wear our Desert Camouflage uniforms with our woodland green combat helmet. At least we are making progress, I thought. Our names had been submitted to supply so that someone could make nametags for our new uniforms. When they arrived they were the same type as those issued to recruits in basic training. These were cheap strips of green cloth which had our names stamped on them in ink. Most of us refused to put these nametags on our new BDU's. Instead we took the nametags, unit patch and rank off one of our woodland BDU's and sewed them to the new uniforms.

29

The Last Mission

It was finally time to turn in equipment. We knew that this was one of the last steps to get back to Germany, but we were conflicted. We had lived in the vehicles training in Germany and in every day since they arrived in Saudi Arabia. We were attached to these vehicles. We knew their unique characteristics. We would no longer have a place to store anything except our duffel bags or rucksacks. The glory machines would be gone forever. When we arrived in Germany our only mission would be to turn in our personal weapons, close the kaserne and give it back to Germany. I felt like I was loosing a friend.

My Bradley had been good to me. It got us wherever we needed to go. It got us out of the front line during the battle when the world was going to hell. It had been the machine that had bruised my body, protected me from the elements, and given me purpose. Once it was gone, what purpose would I have? I would still have the men and we would still need to get back to Germany. But that was such a simple mission. All my men were combat veterans thoroughly accustomed to checking their personal equipment and making sure they were where they were supposed to be. *No one* would miss movement *this time*. I knew that once the Bradley was turned in our cohesion as a unit would begin to come apart.

We were told to write down all the deficiencies of each vehicle so that parts could be ordered and the vehicles worked on as they sat in storage. The officers reminded us that one day we might be returning to these same vehicles and encouraged us to make sure we did a thorough job. After we did our part the mechanics came and inspected the vehicles and ordered parts. Anything that could be fixed immediately was corrected. All of our small equipment that had been brought over in conexes was cleaned and inspected for deficiencies. These were then put into conexes. All of the weapons except for our personal weapons were given a thorough cleaning and inspection. Then they were turned in to the armorer and loaded into another conex.

The next day we were given the route to the prepositioned equipment storage location. We put the Bradleys in a line on the road just outside the assembly area. I looked around to see the area for the last time. The star was now empty except for the mortar tracks and they were getting ready to move. Now we would have no place to return and no Bradleys once they were turned in. The sense of loss was overwhelming. Yes we were leaving after almost five months in the desert, but now we were like refugees. We had no home, no transportation, no purpose except to get back to Germany. Leaving had been a long time coming.

As we rolled along I remembered how excited the men had been when the war was over and wondering when we would be going home. The men were excited about leaving now, but it was tempered by the fact that we were the last unit to redeploy. Only a few military police units would be left. For me there was little to be excited about. I had no one to return to in Germany. Who knew when we would get leave to go home? Where would I go next, now that the unit would no longer exist? Would I know anyone there? My future was full of uncertainty.

As we neared the site I was awestruck. Row upon row of M1A1 tanks and Bradley fighting vehicles were parked side by side on the desert, each one covered with a tarp to help keep the sand at bay. I had seen a lot of armored vehicles parked in motor pools in Germany and the US, but never in this volume. There must have been every tank and Bradley in the Third Armored Division parked in one place. A ground guide directed us where to park in this armored parking lot. Only enough space for a man to walk was left between vehicles.

We grabbed our duffel bags and put them on the sand behind the Bradley. I crawled back inside and took a last look around, looking for anything that we might have left behind. As I looked around the empty turret I found a pair of sunglasses under the radio mount. I chuckled to myself about how funny it would be leave them there for the next crew. Then I remembered how bright outside the sun could make the desert and decided I might need them. I tucked them into my shirt pocket and had a sudden feeling of loss.

Chamberlain called that the truck was just down the row and not waiting on anyone. I climbed out the back door and locked it. Then I helped Chamberlain tie down the tarp to the top of the Bradley. As I walked to the back of the Bradley the truck was just pulling to the adjacent Bradley. I walked over to my duffle bags and shoved them onto the back of the truck then found a spot on the wooden bench seat.

As we pulled away from this massive assemblage of armored combat vehicles I lost sight of my Bradley. It melted into the row like just another loaf of bread on a bakery shelf. That night we stayed in some tents near the mess tent at the headquarters assembly area. It was so nice to have a *hot* meal again. We actually had to let it cool down a little before we could eat the food. Small hardships like this bond combat soldiers in a way noncombat soldiers will seldom experience.

30

Leaving Paradise

It was so nice to have desert camouflage uniforms like everyone else. This time we didn't stand out like I did the last time I was in the headquarters assembly area. We were all in good spirits, but no one acted like the excited youngsters of two and a half months earlier. There was a maturity in their faces, in their stride and in their talk. I couldn't believe these were the same men who had deployed with me just five months earlier. I recalled the scared young men in the days prior to deployment drinking, balking at orders and fighting each other.

Our deployment, the war and months in the desert had brought these young boys into manhood. I was very proud of them. I wondered if their friends and family would notice the change. I doubted it. Around our family and friends we would never have the stature and intimate knowledge that we now had with each other. Whenever I think of them I see their faces and a sense of pride wells inside me. My face naturally breaks into a smile of friendship bonded by war. Parents and friends will never experience this of their soldier even if they live with them the rest of their lives. You had to be there.

As we walked up the stairs into the 747 jet it felt good that we would be arriving in Germany in our new desert camouflage BDU's. We would now stand out from the soldiers who didn't deploy. I never looked back as I got to the top of the stairs. We had been in the Middle East much too long. I looked back in my memory to the time shortly after the war when most of the platoon thought we would be leaving in a few days. It was now about three months later. I was numb.

I just wanted to see green grass and trees again. I just wanted to sit down to a nice restaurant meal and be treated like a normal person. I just wanted to put on civilian clothes and walk downtown. I wanted to get between clean sheets on a real bed and watch TV till my eyes blurred. I just wanted to take a shower anytime I wanted. I wanted to drive my car again. I guess there were a lot of things I wanted to do.

Most of us slept or rested most of the trip. We wanted to be well rested when we hit Germany. Once we were over European air space and closer to Germany I began to get anxious. How would the Germans receive us? Would there be anyone at the airport? Would we get a party when we arrived back in Gelnhausen? I suddenly remembered that there would be no one there to greet me. I had no family, no close friends, no wife or girlfriend. Sure, there were other guys in the platoon in similar circumstances. But I was sure the last thing they would want to do was spend more time with me and vise versa. Seeing the guys with families hug their wives and girlfriends when we arrived would be too much for me to bear. It would only reinforce the fact that I had no one. I decided to walk as fast as I could and avoid eye contact.

As we prepared for landing I craned my neck to see Germany. As usual there were clouds blanketing much of the country. I had hardly seen a cloud in five months. As we broke through the clouds the deepest, darkest green I had ever seen greeted my eyes. My eyes drank in the green foliage like a sponge absorbs water. Almost everyone on board broke into a noisy, excited chatter.

Even the heavy sleepers didn't sleep through this one. As the wheels touched down on the tarmac of Frankfort International Airport we all cheered and clapped. We had waited so long to get back to Germany. The elation of the moment was overwhelming.

As the 747 rolled to our gate I flashed back to the first time I arrived in Germany in 1980. Back then I was a young scared private moving into the unknown. Today I was a Staff Sergeant returning from a victorious war into a country I knew well. I was no longer anxious. Germany had a familiarity that made me feel good. I knew things would be OK. Even though my life was full of unanswered questions I knew they would all be answered in due time. I was out of that horrible desert and that was all I needed to know.

Epilogue

During Operation Desert Shield and Desert Storm the coalition destroyed 3,700 battle tanks, 2,600 artillery pieces, and 2,400 other armored vehicles. Additionally, forty-two Iraqi divisions were made combat ineffective, and 71,204 prisoners were captured according to the U.S. Department Of Defense. This victory was secured as much by the American people as it was by those who fought the war. Without the modernization of equipment, better training, and high standards for enlistment started during the Reagan administration, we could not have had the most lopsided victory in history.

As you have seen, my unit and many others spent many months waiting to return from the Middle East. Most of that time we had no mission, so we languished there while others got the glory. I know that we could have been deployed back to Germany much sooner. It was again just a matter of political will. More planes could have been allocated to get soldiers out of that desert faster. We felt like we had been forgotten and were unappreciated. It should be the policy of this nation that it get its soldiers back to their posts as soon as possible after a conflict, no matter what it takes.

As you have also seen we combat soldiers got a raw deal on many levels. This has been true throughout history. Combat soldiers know they will endure hardships other soldiers in the rear areas won't. However, combat soldiers should never be treated poorly when it comes to the allocation of uniforms, especially when they are deployed from a forest environment to a desert environment. **No one** in these conditions should get these uniforms before the combat soldiers. Combat soldiers see the enemy first, bleed first and die first. Due consideration should then be given to these soldiers. Their lives may depend on them not being seen by the enemy. Some civilian in the rear areas should **never** get these uniforms before all soldiers, combat or otherwise, get them. As a nation we need to make this a priority. Combat soldiers do not ask for much. We can at least let them have new uniforms first.

As with other wars, I believe a memorial should be built to honor those who died in this conflict. The limited number of dead on this memorial will be in stark contrast to other war memorials. The memorial will stand as a reminder that the country does not need years of suffering or thousands of casualties to win a military victory.

Finally, I believe our nation has an obligation to honor its commitments and promises. For a nation as great as ours to sit idly by with a large victorious army while a people fight a lopsided war against an oppressive government is unconscionable. The people of Basra deserved better. The mass graves we found during Operation Iraqi Freedom attest to the brutality of the Iraqi army and the callousness of our inaction. I dream about the faces I saw at the checkpoint and wonder how many of their lives ended in these graves. Will the people of Basra ever forgive us? Will they ever be able to forgive me? I haven't yet been able to forgive myself.

Table of Military Terms

Short Timers: Soldiers who have written orders in hand to leave the unit.

PCS: Permanent Change of Station

ETS: End Time in Service

Day Room: A room set aside in the barracks for single soldiers to relax, watch television, and play games. Can sometimes be used for classes.

Gunnery: Combat units travel to live fire ranges where real ammo is used to practice skills at engaging simulated targets.

Rear Detachment: A group of soldiers designated to stay behind when a unit is deployed. These soldiers may have restricted duty because of wounds or needed to take care of mail delivery, etc.

CQ: (Charge of Quarters) This is a soldier designated to answer the phones, check the security of the Arms Room, and handle minor problems while the unit is off duty. This soldier has a subordinate assigned to him who assists the CQ in his duties.

Conexes: These large metal boxes are used to transport items to be shipped long distances. The sides, top and bottom are made of corrugated steel and have doors on one side that can be padlocked for security. The smallest ones are about 8 feet square.

Platoon Sergeant: The highest-ranking Noncommissioned Officer in a platoon of about thirty soldiers. Only the Platoon Leader outranks the Platoon Sergeant within the platoon.

0-595-33430-X

12520834R00099

Printed in Great Britain
by Amazon